THE CHALLENGE OF
CHANGE

THE CHALLENGE OF
CHANGE

A guide to shaping change and
changing the shape of church

PHIL POTTER

Published by
The Bible Reading Fellowship
15 The Chambers, Vineyard
Abingdon OX14 3FE
United Kingdom
Tel: +44 (0)1865 319700
Email: enquiries@brf.org.uk
Website: www.brf.org.uk
BRF is a Registered Charity

ISBN 978 1 84101 604 7
First published 2009
Reprinted 2010
10 9 8 7 6 5 4 3 2 1
All rights reserved

Acknowledgments
Unless otherwise stated, scripture quotations are taken from the Holy Bible,
New International Version, copyright © 1973, 1978, 1984 by International Bible
Society, are used by permission of Hodder & Stoughton Publishers, a division
of Hodder Headline Ltd. All rights reserved. 'NIV' is a registered trademark of
International Bible Society. UK trademark number 1448790.

Scriptures quoted from the Good News Bible published by The Bible Societies/
HarperCollins Publishers Ltd, UK © American Bible Society 1966, 1971, 1976,
1992, used with permission.

Page 44: Poem taken from Don Everts, *Jesus with Dirty Feet*, copyright © 1999 by
Don Everts and InterVarsity Christian Fellowship/USA, used with permission of
InterVarsity Press, PO Box 1400, Downers Grove, IL 61515, USA. ivpress.com

A catalogue record for this book is available from the British Library

Printed in Singapore by Craft Print International Ltd

CONTENTS

FOREWORD

Change is not to be feared; it is an opportunity provided by the Holy Spirit, who is the Church's overall leader in mission. But when I began ordained ministry, 37 years ago, it was still possible to believe that church leadership was about continuity, not primarily about change. Most churches did their evangelism through their pastoral care. The influence of Christendom seemed strong, many non-churchgoers had a fair idea of the gospel story, and enough people approached the church for 'hatch, match or dispatch' to ensure that Sunday attendance could appear reasonable. It took a particularly inept minister to shrink a church. All of that has changed, as has Western culture. It now takes an exceptional minister to prevent decline.

Perhaps a third of adults in the UK attend church at least occasionally and mostly expect the inherited model. Another third are now 'dechurched', having declined involvement in church as they knew it. Yet another third have never been part of any church and, as yet, have seen no good reason why they should be. The parallel figures for children and youth are much scarier.

If we are to be a mission-shaped church, leaders will have no alternative but to face the challenge of change, while also ensuring appropriate continuity. One size of church can no longer fit all. The practice of leadership has to change, too. Many of us were trained to be pastor–teachers. As Phil Potter shows, our new missionary context now requires us to be poet–gardeners as well.

This excellent book is the fruit of hard-won lessons in leadership and change, mostly learned as a local vicar with a pioneering spirit. Whether you are involved in an inherited model of church, in fresh expressions of church, or in both, you will find help here.

+*Graham Cray*

Introduction

ALL CHANGE!

As if it wasn't enough being squeezed like a canned sardine inside a London tube train at rush hour, the change options coming over the tannoy were taking my sense of disorientation to a whole new level.

'Change here for southbound Northern Line service via Bank from platform six, Victoria Line, and mainline inner-city and suburban rail services…'

It may have been a perfectly clear and understandable announcement for a seasoned Londoner but, for the average traveller, it was a tad confusing. Of course, if I'd remembered to pack just one of my many London tube maps, or happened to be standing in front of one, I'm sure it would have been very straightforward. But without a map and with a heaving throng of impatient commuters pushing from behind, the change options became ever more confusing and the stress levels kept rising… three tunnels to choose from, no, four, with several more turning points along the way. Five minutes later, I was sitting on the wrong train on the wrong seat, staring at the wrong scenery, and going in the wrong direction. Ironically, I was thinking about writing this book at the time, and about whether my impending change of job might change my intention to write, and whether I needed to negotiate a change of timescale in the contract. Oh, and I was also visiting my daughter, who happened to be changing career and wondering whether to change churches as well as changing where she lived.

Change can feel uncomfortable and risky, but it invades our lives at every level. As a friend of mine used to say, 'constant change is here to stay'. If he was alive today, he'd now have to replace the word 'constant' with the word 'increasing'. Change is a dominant force in our lives and it will always have a dominating effect on how we view and tackle our world.

This book is about how we view and tackle the Church in the light of change. Down in the underground I found myself unprepared and ultimately overwhelmed in an unfamiliar place, and that led to a few wrong turns and bad choices. Five minutes later, of course, I was back on the right train and on the right track, but in the Church our choices and turns can make or break the future. Decisions on what and how and when we change will not only affect growth or decline in a church but, most importantly, they will impact people. Too often it is people who are left damaged and disillusioned by the impact—congregations who couldn't catch the vision, individuals who were left bewildered and bereft, and leaders who ended up burnt out by their attempts to bring about healthy and godly change.

What I'd like to do here is to offer a map for change. In the same way as a London tube map is simplified into colour-coded options, joining up at various points and highlighting the available routes, I simply want to provide a practical guide. It doesn't attempt to navigate the thousands of tunnels you'll encounter along the way, but it does set out to mark the stations and routes, the options and principles of change that will take us to a new and better future. As I write, I'm imagining a church leader who wants to take his or her congregation on a change journey, or a whole church either preparing to embark on a particular project or simply wanting to be envisioned and equipped for what lies ahead. I also imagine a wide selection of readers, from the impatient visionary to the reluctant traditionalist, from the energized leader to the broken pastor, and from large and thriving churches to small and struggling congregations.

With this in mind, I write very much as a pastor and practitioner, and have included over 100 questions for practical reflection and group discussion. These questions are not meant to be slavishly worked through one by one, but are there simply as a tool to help you identify and focus on the issues that are most relevant for you at the present time, and the areas that need to be addressed as a priority. This may also mean that you cover a single chapter's material in each session, or that you return to the same chapter more than once.

The book is broken into two halves. The first half is intended as a practical manual for shaping change of any kind in the life of a church. The second half is a guide to understanding the changing shape of church, and in particular the 'Fresh Expressions' of church that are now emerging. In this sense, the subject matter is fairly wide-ranging and can therefore be either read selectively or progressively. Chapter One, on 'shaping up', for instance, applies to every Christian believer and challenges our general resistance to change. By Chapter Six, however, thoughts about structural change may offer a challenge to some of our more senior church leaders.

Finally, what qualifies and inspires me to write on this subject? Well, nearly 30 years ago, I was taken on board and in hand by one of the most influential change agents of the late 20th century. David Watson was then leading one of the most exciting churches in the UK, at St Michael-le-Belfry in York. He recruited me to lead his team of singers, dancers and actors, and together we travelled internationally, encouraging renewal, promoting unity and modelling new ways of engaging in evangelism. I was a singer-songwriter and worship leader, writing and pioneering new ideas for worship alongside our more traditional hymns and liturgy. Singing rhythmic songs with the additional diet of dance and drama was a seismic change for some of the cathedrals and churches we visited. In one cathedral, we built our theme around some lines from Bob Dylan's song 'Ballad of a Thin Man': 'Something is happening here, but you don't know what it is, do you, Mister Jones?' Only after the service did we discover that the sub dean of the cathedral was called Mr Jones. The early 1980s were exciting days for the renewal of the Church. Many of the changes that we now take for granted were pioneered in that era by godly risk-taking leaders. As a worship leader, I sat at the feet of many of them and was privileged to look, listen and learn.

I then entered the ordained ministry and served as a curate in

St Peter's, Yateley, a church that had had its building burnt down by an arsonist. This dramatic event had not only left the church with the chance to rebuild from scratch but had given them a sense of spiritual rebirth and rediscovery. It led to a period of ongoing change and development, of which I was a part, and a time of astonishing growth. When it was discovered that the arsonist had burnt down other churches, which had also then seen renewal, the suggestion was made that he should be released from prison and given a ministry and a list!

Four years later, our family moved to a traditional, urban community in Haydock on Merseyside, and so began a ministry lasting nearly 20 years in the parish of St Mark's. Of course, I'm often asked why somebody who likes to do change did not change his place of ministry for that length of time. My answer is that St Mark's went through five major transitions during that time, changes that effectively gave me the feel of leading five refreshingly different churches. The first phase was simply *renewal*, where the foundations of worship, community and mission were reviewed and developed. This included a review of all our resources, including our buildings, and led to a major phase of *reordering*. The biggest reordering, of course, was in people's hearts and expectations, and the ministry and growth that this released led to a period of *restructuring* and the advent of cell church. Over a period of six months, we overhauled our programmes, groups and structures and began to embrace the cell motto that 'small is beautiful'. The resulting growth and blessing gave us an appetite and a very clear call for *resourcing* others. Not only did we host conferences and welcome visiting leaders but we began to look for ways to team up with others and offer our gifts more widely.

Eventually, we grew to four congregations, but I was haunted by two thoughts. First of all, it's easy in a full building to become complacent and feel successful, when the reality is that there are still 10,000 people on our doorstep who never venture inside and for whom we are still irrelevant. The second thought followed quickly, that if any church was in a position to take risks and experiment in reaching the totally unchurched, it was a community like St Mark's, since by now we had learnt some powerful, if sometimes painful lessons about the importance of ongoing change. So we then entered our riskiest and most exciting transition of all, and we called it *reinventing*. This involved loosening our hold on all our programme-driven services, groups and events, and led to several groups of people moving out into completely new contexts, where the shape of church could be allowed to evolve in new and exciting ways.

Since then, I have entered another change phase of my own, which I call *releasing*. After many years in the parish, I have now taken up the post of Director of Pioneer Ministry in the diocese of Liverpool. Put very simply, I've been told that my job is to 'illustrate the future'. With a team of pioneer ministers and an ever-increasing army of lay pioneers, we are doing church in new ways alongside the old ways, and beginning to imagine and then illustrate how tomorrow's church might look.

At times, I must confess, it all feels a little like the London tube experience. Not only are there several possible routes, but also a lot of tunnels and one or two cul de sacs along the way. And then, of course, there are several voices coming over the tannoy, all suggesting different stations. Around it all, there's a heaving, pushing mass called 'the unchurched', who are often sick of the Church but still hungry for God. My greatest conviction, however, is that we are definitely on the right train and heading in the right direction. I also hope you'll agree, as you travel these pages, that for followers of Jesus there is nothing more important or fulfilling than the challenge of change.

Chapter One

✠

SHAPING UP: THE PATH TO CHANGE

Forget the former things; do not dwell on the past. See, I am doing a new thing! Now it springs up; do you not perceive it? I am making a way in the desert and streams in the wasteland.
ISAIAH 43:18–19

This was the very first motto verse I introduced at St Mark's as a fresh young vicar. I was sure the church was ready for new things because they'd said so in their parish profile. In fact, the document was so full of high expectations that any candidate might be forgiven for concluding that the church wanted only Jesus himself to apply for the post. (A careful read, however, would also confirm that he would never have been appointed because he wasn't married with two children!) Even so, it seemed obvious that, with such a list of expectations, here was a church ready for change. I was offered the job and took it.

The motto verse was introduced and Isaiah was preached, and the first opportunity for change appeared in the worship on Pentecost Sunday. Having come from York, I had a very high view of Pentecost as one of the most important festivals of the year, a time for renewal and rededication, and an ideal occasion for marking new beginnings. I came also with the memory of waves of people receiving the laying on of hands, streaming forward to embrace any and every offer of further blessing and spiritual strength. So I preached on the new thing that God was doing at Pentecost and invited people to come forward to receive prayer through the laying on of hands. It was all done very carefully, gently and sensitively in the context of Communion, so people could respond after receiving the bread and the wine, without feeling pressurized or threatened in any way. My wife and I knelt together at the upper rail and we waited for the waves. We waited and prayed and waited some more and continued to wait for some time after, until even we were embarrassed.

Now, nearly 20 years later, the whole culture of receiving prayer ministry in the context of worship has massively changed. It is now the norm for people not only to respond but to respond continually and in several ways. It happens through teams of people praying before and after services and during Communion, and it also happens after most sermons in most services. The church culture itself has changed so that people of all ages and every taste and temperament understand it, expect it and collectively embrace it.

So what changed? The answer is 'a great deal over a long period of time', and over the next few chapters we'll explore some of the more practical principles from the journey. But the very first lesson that I had to learn, with all my new ideas, was that before we could see the culture change, we needed to see a climate change. The truth here was that there was an ingrained resistance in the church that had nothing to do with opposing the ideas or the vision itself, or even the way in which it was presented to people. The problem was a deeper one and far more fundamental. What was needed before anything else was a change of heart. As the saying goes, 'The heart of the human problem is the problem of the human heart'.

I've heard and preached many an evangelistic sermon on this saying, but it's just as true for the Church of God as it is for the cynical unbeliever. The problem with any change is not primarily about resources, traditions, communication or even understanding, but about the heart, and at the heart of the 'change' problem is the problem of changing hearts. Over the years, I've learnt as a pastor to put this at the top of our change agenda, which is why it's introduced here in Chapter One.

My first significant lesson in this area was in leading the church into a major building project. As we set out, we applied some very helpful and practical principles that you'll find in the following two chapters. We prayed, discussed and debated, consulted, explained and communicated, and eventually we agreed clearly and unanimously to move ahead. Everything was now in place, and we were ready for our first major gift day. Or were we? Two months beforehand, I went to Tanzania for two weeks to teach at a clergy conference, leaving a keen and buzzing congregation preparing for the launch. When I returned, I couldn't believe how quickly the mood had changed across the church, as I was met with wave after wave of confusion, anger and a toxic fear that was quickly beginning to spread.

Immediately I cancelled everything in my diary and began to visit people. I tried to go well armed with the arguments and assurances that had already been carefully worked through and agreed. I thought, 'If they know in their heads what I now know, they'll see it all clearly and come on board.' Fortunately, that thought was overtaken by the far more important one, that 'people don't care what you know till they know that you care', and so I went primarily as their pastor to listen. To my amazement, I encountered the very same experience every time. The visit would begin with a barrage of issues about the project and why they were now against it, but within half an hour the conversation had shifted well beyond the building issues to issues of the heart, which had nothing whatsoever to do with the challenge of changing buildings. In essence, the challenge of change itself had stirred up deeper hurts, fears, pride and prejudice that needed dealing with before anything else could happen. The very move toward making history by transforming the building was causing people to remember history—whom they'd fallen out with, the roles they were never given, needs that were never met.

We put the building project aside for a while and worked on these issues of the heart, restoring relationships, addressing personal needs and working through unfulfilled expectations. The lesson I'll never forget is that as each of these deeper issues was dealt with, the building problems evaporated and became irrelevant. One month later and the whole church gave a resounding 'yes' to the project, with an amazing gift day that raised nearly 20 times the expected amount.

In hindsight, I shouldn't have been so surprised. The renewal of buildings, services, groups and programmes is always preceded by a renewal of the heart. Around the time of our own building project, I read and re-read George Carey's book *The Church in the Market Place*. Halfway through his congregation's project, it came to a grinding halt, and he writes:

It was clear then that grievous as the Council's decision was, God was telling us something so clearly that we would have been spiritually stone-deaf to have misunderstood. He was saying 'I am more interested in you than a fine building. Unless you are renewed, a lovely place is beside the point. When you are made alive then I will bring this thing to pass.'[1]

What is required to make us alive and alert to the changes our churches need? The Old Testament prophets were specialists in spiritual change. While they were not always the most sensitive change agents, they were cuttingly clear in communicating the word of God. Isaiah has often been called the prince of prophets, and I've found myself returning to his words when trying to communicate the heart of change: 'Forget the former things; do not dwell on the past. See, I am doing a new thing!' Reflecting on the lessons I've learnt about changing hearts, there are six things in particular that seem essential in changing a church's spiritual climate, all illustrated in the life and times of Isaiah.

A NEW HONESTY

Under C in *Bacon Sandwiches and Salvation: an A–Z of the Christian Life*, Adrian Plass offers the following entry:

Change: rare phenomenon as far as the church is concerned, except when it comes to the collection. Tends to be fairly limited even then.[2]

There is no shortage of jokes around when people reflect on change and the lack of it in many churches. Inside those churches there is no shortage of excuses for not changing. Here's a list that someone compiled and I've extended.

- We've always done it that way in this church.
- We've never done it that way in this church.
- I'm sure it's not God's will.
- You'll upset/offend your mother/father/minister/children/friends/bishop.
- It's too ambitious/soon/far/quick/new/different.
- We're too old/young/inexperienced/set in our ways.
- It will cost too much.
- It's not professional enough.
- Folk will not understand/appreciate/support/listen.
- We've tried that before.
- We haven't the time/resources/people/gifts.
- We're not ready for it yet.
- Interesting idea, but our church is different.
- All right in theory, but can you put it into practice?
- It's against our tradition/policy/doctrine.
- It needs more research/study/investigation.
- Somebody would have suggested it before if it were any good.
- Let's discuss it at another time.
- You don't understand our problem…
- We have too many things going on now.
- Let's be practical.
- Let's form a committee.
- Let's shelve it for the time being.
- Let's get back to reality.
- Who do you think you are?

The trouble is that beneath the humour lie some serious issues and uncomfortable truths. Gordon Bailey sums it up starkly in his poem 'Granite Choir'.

No wonder the graveyards and tombstones have spread
To where the pews echo the chants of the dead.
Decay marks the windows, the arches, the walls,
And granite-faced statues sit in the choir stalls.
They seem to have fossils where hearts ought to be
Their stoney-hard minds knowing nothing of me.[3]

It's a bleaker picture than most, perhaps, and anyone reading this book will be hoping their church looks nothing like this. But it's the phrase 'where hearts ought to be' that bites, and the picture of a church so fossilized that it's incapable of relating to anyone outside its walls. What is most disturbing, however, is that churches that are not in touch with the heart often perceive themselves in a completely different way, believing that they are open, flexible and perfectly healthy. In fact, someone has likened the Church to an equestrian statue, a horse portrayed in the very act of leaping forward with its mane flowing and muscles rippling. Whether you come back in ten years or 200 years, it won't have moved a fraction of an inch. My fear is that the Church is very good at appearing to move and consider change, especially through initiatives like the Decade of Evangelism, Fresh Expressions and countless other mission ventures, but the pace at which it moves is still frighteningly slower than the pace of our world.

Isaiah's words, 'See, I am doing a new thing', reflect the fact that God, by his very nature, is a God of movement. He never stands still but delights in doing new things in people's lives. He is the God of the new song, the new heart, the new name, the new covenant, the new creation, and the new heaven and earth. The writer of Lamentations wrote: 'Because of the Lord's great love we are not consumed, for his compassions never fail. They are new every morning; great is your faithfulness' (Lamentations 3:22–23). In other words, he is a faithful God who never changes, the rock who is always the same, yesterday, today and for ever—but he is dealing with an imperfect people who constantly need changing and moving on. Every day and every week of every month of every year, there are new things that I and my church can learn about God and his compassionate ways, and new responses for us to make.

All this has to begin with a new honesty, and, if we are not to cling to the past, we can certainly learn from it, as Isaiah was keen for his audience to do. The Danish philosopher Søren Kirkegaard rightly said, 'Life can only be understood backwards; but it must be lived forwards', and Isaiah encouraged people to be honest about their past. God had delivered them from the slavery of Egypt and they'd journeyed into the wilderness with great joy and praise. However, instead of reaching the promised land in about 40 days, it took them 40 years, because of their rebellion and unbelief and their enormous capacity to grumble at any sign of change. Even when they did arrive, they ultimately refused to go the whole way with God, continued to rebel and ended up in exile. Isaiah's prophecy takes these events in the past and looks forward to the day when the nation will be led out of exile and, beyond that, when the Messiah will come and give them a new future.

Tragically, when Jesus did come and died on the cross, God's people still didn't recognize what God was doing; they were still too busy rebelling and grumbling. That is a powerful parable of many churches today, of people who have been set free from sin and are being led into the promised land of God's grace. Wherever the Church is too busy being rebellious and unbelieving, it fails to see what God is doing and misses out on the fullness of his promises. Meanwhile, our churches can end up taking 40 years to develop something that should only take three or four at the most, going round and round in circles and failing to look and live forwards.

Any change process, then, must begin with a brutal honesty about where we really are at the moment. Over the years, I have often found the following self-examination questions helpful, offered by David Watson in *I Believe in Evangelism*.

- *At least once a year, ruthless questions need to be asked in an attitude of prayer and submission to God about the whole pattern of our services, our meetings and organizations and buildings.*
- *Are they achieving anything today?*
- *Are they the best use of time and money today?*
- *Are they helping to build up the Body of Christ today?*
- *Are they assisting the church in evangelism today?*
- *Are they God's best plan for today?*

Their value yesterday is not the important point. Christian work is constantly crippled by clinging to blessings and traditions of the past. God is not the God of yesterday. He is the God of today... heaven forbid that we should continue playing religious games in one corner when the cloud and fire of God's presence have moved to another.[4]

A NEW HUMILITY

How do we see and discern when and where God is moving? How do we see when and where and what to change? In Isaiah 6 we find a powerful answer, as the prophet himself undergoes a personal change when he sees the King of kings. The lesson from his encounter before God's throne is that we cannot understand anything in spiritual terms until we draw close to the King himself, and we cannot and should not trust ourselves to make any judgments about change outside the context of worship and seeking God's face.

In fact, the closeness of Isaiah's encounter reminds me of the story of an Anglican vicar and a Baptist minister who were great rivals in the town. They both died on the same day and arrived in heaven. The vicar was delighted to see thousands of Anglicans gathered directly around the throne of God. Beyond them, in an outer circle, were the Catholics, and then came the Methodists, Pentecostals and Presbyterians. The circles stretched a long, long way, but far beyond them all and over the horizon were the Baptists. 'So what do you make of that?' said the vicar in triumph, but the Baptist seemed quite happy with the arrangement. 'Aren't you shocked?' asked the vicar. 'Not at all,' he replied. 'I've just had a word with the archangel and apparently mine are the only lot that God can trust out of his sight!'

Isaiah would have identified with that, because when he ended up in front of the throne and saw the glory of God, he knew in an instant that he could never be trusted anywhere else. He needed to be directly in front of the throne, at the centre of God's mercy and grace, to have any chance of being the man he was meant to be. Before that, of course, he had had the outward appearance of being a model believer and leader. He was always in the temple, continually praying and preaching and proclaiming his faith, but as soon as he saw the king he discovered a new humility. He discovered that when you start to see God as he really is, you immediately see yourself as you really are. As you begin to see God's glory, you also begin to recognize your own weakness—and there are three weaknesses in particular that Isaiah saw, and that we need to see to be freed for lasting change.

The first is *self-justification*. The background to Isaiah's story is King Uzziah's story in 2 Chronicles 26. He was a man who started out as a God-fearing king, who 'sought the Lord' (v. 5) and prospered, becoming strong and powerful, but eventually 'his pride led to his downfall' (v. 16). He arrogantly took over the high priest's role and went into the Holy of Holies, the inner sanctuary of the temple, to offer his own act of worship, and the story ends with Uzziah contracting leprosy, remaining 'leprous and excluded' (v. 21) until the day he died. The question now was what would happen to the nation of Judah. Would a strong and godly king take over or would the downward slide continue?

It was a critical moment in the nation's history, and it was Isaiah's job, as the number one prophet, to speak into the situation. What was God going to show him about the need for change? Isaiah would have seen enough pride and arrogance in Uzziah to warn everybody else against it and, judging from his pronouncements before Isaiah 6, you can imagine what he was likely to say: 'I, the anointed royal prophet, blameless servant of God, blame the king for all our problems, so watch out that you don't become like him!' In fact, in the first five chapters of his book there are five sermons of woes and warnings on everybody but Isaiah himself. However, after a single glance at God's glory in chapter 6, he now declares: 'Woe to me! … I am ruined! For I am a man of unclean lips, and I live among a people of unclean lips, and my eyes have seen the King, the Lord Almighty' (Isaiah 6:5).

Personally I prefer the old King James translation: 'I am undone.' The fact is that, whenever I come in prayer with any attitude or complaint or even a vision that is not of God, then very quickly 'I am undone', and before long I realize that my thoughts and motives have been totally inappropriate. The secret is, of course, to come to God with an open heart, allowing him to weigh our motives and our readiness to move with him.

Looking back at the major change periods in the churches I've belonged to, I'd have to say that all the prayer gatherings have been key, and especially the half-nights of prayer. Many times we would gather as a church with a shopping list of requests and reasons for our vision, and every time the focus would shift from self-justification to personal change and transformation. When the church responded to this focus, it swiftly saw where God was leading and what he actually wanted to change. Robert Murray McCheyne, a famous 19th-century Scottish pastor, once said to his congregation, 'Here's a phrase and I want you to complete it with your own ending.' Then he said, 'The greatest need of my church is…' and the people wrote their answers. I imagine that those answers may have been very similar to the answers we hear in our own churches today: 'Our greatest need is for more resources, more gifts, more commitment, more stability and tradition.' But McCheyne's answer was this: 'The greatest need of my church is my personal holiness.' He went on to say, 'It's not great talents that God blesses, but great likeness to Jesus.' It's very easy to try to justify our own opinions and plans, but far better in the long run to be justified by him.

The second weakness that Isaiah perceived was his *self-exaltation*. He saw it the moment he saw the seraphim, because these creatures surrounding the throne were veiling themselves, hiding their own features: 'with two wings they covered their faces, with two they covered their feet, and with two they were flying' (v. 2). They did this because, although they must have been awesome to watch, the one upon the throne was infinitely more so, and they were concerned lest they should in any way detract from the majesty of the King. So they hid themselves with four of their wings, and only used two for their task. That must have had a profound effect on Isaiah because, in a sense, he'd been using all his wings to display himself and his ministry: preaching, teaching, prophesying, leading, serving, working. In effect, his role and position had perhaps been more important to him than his relationship with the King.

Role plays a powerful part in the life of the church, and it can cause havoc when change is in the air. I remember that as people queued up to greet us on the evening of my induction to St Mark's, the majority introduced themselves by their role and not by their name: lay reader, Sunday school teacher, treasurer, ladies' group leader and so on. It probably wasn't surprising, then, that in the early days of my ministry there people clung tenaciously to their role, and often saw any suggestion of change as a direct threat to it. Without a whole and secure relationship with God and with one another, role soon takes the ascendancy, and that can be dangerously true of the person in overall charge. Many churches see little change because their minister clings on to the security of his or her role. Every-member ministry can feel like a threat to his authority, open worship a threat to her calling as priest, and honest and vulnerable relationships a threat to the position of senior pastor. Any change process is stifled if self-exaltation and the importance of role play a dominant part.

The third weakness from which Isaiah needed liberating was *self-*

preservation. What is striking here is that, as soon as he had been touched and forgiven, he abandoned himself and his service to the will of God: 'Then I heard the voice of the Lord saying, "Whom shall I send? And who will go for us?" And I said, "Here I am. Send me!"' (v. 8). Of course, God could never utter those words until Isaiah had a change of heart. When God does begin to touch us, he automatically ends up with people who are open and ready for change. Self-preservation can be a huge problem in the management of change in a church. We all tend to search for a place of safety and security, and once we think we have found it, it's difficult to let go. Maybe that's why it's been said that organizations begin with a man, then become a movement, that develops into a machine, that eventually turns into a monument. Movements are exciting and energizing, which is why, perhaps, we soon feel the need to protect them with our machines, which inevitably degenerate into monuments. The only antidote is not to try to preserve them at all, but to hand them continually on an open palm back to God.

A NEW HUNGER

Once we begin to be more honest and humble, then the hunger sets in. It's the same progression that we see in the Beatitudes:

Blessed are the poor in spirit,
for theirs is the kingdom of heaven.
Blessed are those who mourn,
for they will be comforted.
Blessed are the meek,
for they will inherit the earth (Matthew 5:3–5).

'Blessed are the meek' has appropriately been paraphrased 'Blessed are those who have a true view of themselves'. For people to be willing to change, they need a true picture of where they really are; only then can they glimpse where they could be. Before our church could embrace renewal, it had to realize that there was so much more to discover and enjoy. So before we renewed the worship, we took people to festivals, conferences and holiday weeks, and showed them what was happening elsewhere. Before we took out the pews and reordered the building, we took them to beautiful churches with comfortable chairs and welcome areas. Similarly, we have welcomed many church groups, staff teams and even coachloads of congregations to St Mark's to see for themselves what God can do. This paves the way for the fourth beatitude: 'Blessed are those who hunger and thirst for righteousness, for they will be filled' (v. 6).

We should never forget that God can only fill those who are hungry. When the psalmist says, 'Taste and see that the Lord is good' (Psalm 34:8), the implication is that looking at food and smelling it is not enough: we gain nourishment only from eating it. And when a church is hungry enough to taste what God has on offer for them, they begin to be fed and then filled with further blessing.

Isaiah appeals repeatedly to this principle. He invites those who are thirsty to 'come to the waters' and to 'eat what is good' (55:1–2). He complains to those who cling to the past that 'you have not called upon me, O Jacob, you have not wearied yourselves for me, O Israel' (43:22). In other words, they have never put themselves out in seeking God or shown any hunger for his blessing. And in chapter 54, Isaiah introduces the image of a tent that needs enlarging and stretching: 'Enlarge the place of your tent, stretch your tent curtains wide, do not hold back; lengthen your cords, strengthen your stakes. For you will spread out to the right and to the left' (vv. 2–3).

I love that image because it reminds me of holidays spent in tents and caravans, where every pitch had its neat little territory with a bush between it and the next one. If we'd started stretching the tent and invading other people's space, then war would have broken out on the campsite. Besides, we were very happy with our own little patch, thank you very much. But it's easy to apply this picture to the Church, too, where so often we are inclined to be satisfied with our own little patch. We feel cosy within our own little fellowship, congregation or ministry, which stays within the boundaries and knows its limitations and revels in the security that that brings. Yet God may be calling us out of that space and telling us to move into a wider territory.

We should remember, though, that the primary image here is one of stretching, and stretching is often painful, which takes us to the next principle in changing the heart.

A NEW KIND OF HURT

Spirituality writer Michel Quoist says, 'I am afraid of the "yes" that entails other "yeses". And yet I am not at peace.'[5] Change of any kind, in any context, is challenging, but the Christian faces a further challenge in the ongoing call to die to self. Jesus said:

'Unless a kernel of wheat falls to the ground and dies, it remains only a single seed. But if it dies, it produces many seeds. Those who love their lives will lose them, while those who hate their lives in this world will keep them for eternal life. Whoever serves me must follow me; and where I am, my servant also will be' (John 12:24–26).

When the Church of England published the report *Mission-Shaped Church* (looking at new ways of doing church), it first had the title *Dying to Live*. The title was dropped because of the potential for a negative media response, but in many ways it was an excellent one. Many of our churches really are dying to live, and most Christians are dying to be able to show their friends, colleagues and neighbours that church can be relevant and life-giving. Before that can happen, though, the phrase should be turned around and embraced in its biblical form as a question: Are we willing to die, in order that we might live? Are we willing to allow some of our convictions about doing church to die as well, so that we and the world we serve can truly live?

Immediately after Isaiah's appeal to 'forget the former things' and see the new, and his complaint about the people's lack of hunger, comes a similar complaint from God about offerings and sacrifices:

You have not brought me sheep for burnt offerings, nor honoured me with your sacrifices. I have not burdened you with grain offerings nor wearied you with demands for incense. You have not bought any fragrant calamus for me, or lavished on me the fat of your sacrifices. But you have burdened me with your sins and wearied me with your offences (Isaiah 43:23–24).

Isaiah's audience had failed to offer any form of genuine worship. Offence to God can take many forms, but the slide toward sin is never more apparent than when our offerings are token and half-hearted, and when they lack the 'sacrificial' element. In fact, our own language makes a clear distinction between what we define as an offering and what we consider a sacrifice. It's well illustrated in the tale of the pig and the chicken, who were walking down the road one day and came across an egg and bacon restaurant. They looked through the windows and saw the appetizing plates of bacon and eggs, and the pig looked very glum, while the chicken looked smug. The pig then said to the chicken, 'Well, it's all very well for you; for you it's an offering, but for me it's a sacrifice!'

You also see the difference when two people get married. First of all, the man may offer his hand and say, 'I'm completely yours.' But then he has to start making one or two sacrifices to make the marriage work, beginning with the forsaking of Sally and Janet and Julie and anyone else in line. Both partners then have to do a lot of other things to keep that marriage alive and developing. Where there is no sacrifice in a marriage, the marriage will eventually die; and, very simply, where there is no sacrifice in the church, the church itself will die. Sadly, there are many churches where the congregations have made a basic offering of weekly worship, but collectively they are not making any sacrifices to make it live and grow and develop. The truth is that any church that wants to stay alive must learn, in the end, to honour God with its sacrifices.

Taking both these analogies, the difference between an offering and a sacrifice is that when you offer a sacrifice, it hurts. When we really listen to God's word, and especially this call to die, our consciences begin to hurt. When we begin to give more of our money to God's work, our pockets will hurt. And when we begin to work together and worship in a way that includes everybody, recognizing that my way isn't necessarily the right or best way, our pride can be hurt. When we also begin to venture out into a broken and hurting world, which happens to be God's world, then our hearts begin to hurt. Sooner or later, we face the truth that the Christian life is a life of sacrifice, and that everything we hold dear in the church must also be held on an open palm before God.

For many of us, if we're honest, this is a new kind of pain that we don't easily take on board. Like people throughout history, our tendency when faced with the pain of change is to start looking back, pining for the former things, clinging to the past, because it is too painful to move on. But God has never promised us absence of pain in this world; in fact, he talks continuously of the opposite. Isaiah 43, where we read about God's promise of a 'new thing', begins with verses announcing his presence with his people 'when you pass through the waters' and 'when you walk through the fire'. He doesn't says 'if' but 'when', and it's only as we begin to embrace this call to endure hardship that we can embrace the blessing. Many churches, however, develop so far and no further because they will not cross the pain threshold of developments, changes and further learning, because of the sacrifices involved. I'm reminded of the poster that shows a rather sad-looking rag doll, with its head passing through an old washing mangle. The caption reads, 'The truth will set you free, but first it will make you miserable'! The truth is that change hurts, but it leads to freedom.

A NEW HARMONY

It should be obvious by now that any church willing to embrace the challenge of change, and engage with it from the heart, will need to value its relationships. If honesty, humility and hurt are all involved, however, then simple agreement will not be enough. A changing church will increasingly need to know how to love one another, accept one another, encourage one another, bear with one another and, most likely, forgive one another. Unfortunately, this often appears as one of the major obstacles to genuine change. You may have heard the rewrite of the hymn 'Onward Christian Soldiers':

Like a mighty tortoise
Moves the Church of God,
Brothers, we are treading
Where we've always trod;
We are all divided,
Many bodies we,
Very strong on doctrine,
Weak on charity.

In so many parts of the Church today, fellowship is impaired through the souring of relationships, a critical spirit, distrust, grumbling, gossiping, divisive and hurtful remarks, along with an array of cliques and competing factions. The dangers are multiplied when a fragile church is grappling with the challenge of change, and Paul's warning to the Galatians rings all too true: 'The entire law is summed up in a single command: "Love your neighbour as yourself." If you keep on biting and devouring each other, watch out or you will be destroyed by each other' (Galatians 5:14–15). These are strong words but salutary ones for any church that is trying to move forward along potentially diverging paths.

In *The Challenge of Cell Church*, I wrote about working long and hard to break down some of the uglier attitudes in our midst and to build up the quality of community and communication.[6] I am now convinced that nothing of any value would have happened in St Mark's if the quality of our relationships had not become an absolute priority, both before and during significant periods of change. This particular value will reappear in some of the remaining chapters of this book.

A NEW HOPE

You may feel that this has been a heavy place to start. Honesty, humility, hunger, hurt and harmony are hugely challenging issues before we ever mention the word 'change', and yet it would probably be dishonest to begin anywhere else. As I have suggested, whenever I have been invited to share a church's journey of change, the heart issues have been a far hotter issue than either the planning or the process, but when the heart is tackled first, the practical problems are resolved with relative ease. There is one other factor, however, that unlocks all the others and makes for a smoother journey, and that is the message of hope that sings out from the Bible's pages.

The book of Isaiah contains some amazing promises of hope, with a particular favourite being this verse from chapter 40:

But those who hope in the Lord
will renew their strength.
They will soar on wings like eagles;
they will run and not grow weary,
they will walk and not be faint (v. 31).

If we are fortunate enough to see an eagle in flight, we will see it rise higher and higher in the sky in ascending circles, without any effort. All it has to do is to flap its wings a few times until it finds a rising column of air, and then it locks its wings into a full spread and relaxes into an upward spiral flight. In contrast, when you and I are faced with some of the challenges in this chapter, we simply get into a flap. What we are meant to do is to lock ourselves into the wind of God's Spirit in worship, allowing ourselves to be carried higher and higher into his presence, where we can begin to see things from his perspective, looking down on the challenges instead of being dragged down by them.

'For my thoughts are not your thoughts,
neither are your ways my ways," declares the Lord.
'As the heavens are higher than the earth,
so are my ways higher than your ways
and my thoughts than your thoughts' (Isaiah 55:8–9).

Think about when boarding a plane and taking off. Immediately the landscape looks very different. The higher you go, the more you can see, and the more different it all looks. Part of Isaiah's message is that the higher you and I rise in our worship and the closer we draw to God, the more different our lives and our churches are going to look, and the more we will see what God wants us to see.

When David Livingstone was called to Africa in the 19th century, he heard another missionary, Dr Robert Moffatt, speak about the land. Dr Moffatt spoke of 'a vast plain to the north where I've sometimes seen, in the morning sun, the smoke of a thousand villages, [where] no missionary has ever been'. This picture haunted Livingstone, especially the words 'the smoke of a thousand villages'. I've been to Africa myself, and the landscapes are awesome. You can stand looking over vast expanses of wilderness with not a sign of life. You can then drive hundreds of miles into that wilderness and eventually come across whole areas that are teeming with life, where literally thousands of zebra and wildebeest and other exotic wildlife congregate. It is an amazing experience. Dr Moffatt must have seen it for himself; only, as he stood and looked, he began to see far on the horizon 'the smoke of a thousand villages'—a thousand thriving communities who had never heard about Christ—and his eyes and heart were opened. Livingstone caught that vision; with others, he went there, and Africa was never the same again.

Not surprisingly, God wants to give you and me exactly the same kind of vision. So often, we look at our lives and the churches around us and we see a wilderness, seemingly empty of hope and spiritual life. As we see it from God's perspective, however, we begin to glimpse, as it were, 'the smoke of a thousand villages'—a thousand ways in which God could move, a thousand opportunities for God to bless, a thousand encouragements to move us toward a significant goal. The following chapters will begin to give us practical tools to reach that goal, equipped now with the principles from this chapter, which focus on the need for a changed heart, a heart that has pondered honesty, humility, hunger, hurt, harmony and hope, before it attempts to change anything.

———— ✣ ————

MEETING THE CHALLENGE

'The heart of the human problem is the problem of the human heart.'

Which of the six heart issues do you feel affects you most?

- Honesty
- Humility
- Hunger
- Hurt
- Harmony
- Hope

Do you feel that any of them in particular may be a problem for your church, and if so, why? On a scale of 1–10, how would your church score on each one?

Honesty

- What do you think is your church's greatest strength and greatest weakness in the way it perceives itself?

Humility

- Self-justification, self-exaltation, self-preservation. Do you recognize any of these in yourself? In your church?
- How is a vision of the King kept central in the life of your church?

Hunger

- What do you think your church is hungry for at the moment?
- How is that hunger being fed?
- What is being done to create more hunger?

Hurt

- What sacrifices are you personally making to keep your church alive and developing?
- What sacrifices has your church collectively made over the last three years?
- What sacrifice, in particular, should it make now in building a new future?

Harmony

- How high a value does your church place on the quality of relationships?
- Are there any unresolved conflicts in the life of the fellowship that could block the path to change?
- What might be done to resolve them?

Hope

- How is hope nurtured in your church?
- What hopes has God given you for your church's future?
- What part does he want you to play in realizing them?

Chapter Two

SHAPING PRIORITIES:
THE PLANNING OF CHANGE

That evening after sunset the people brought to Jesus all the sick and de-mon-possessed. The whole town gathered at the door, and Jesus healed many who had various diseases. He also drove out many demons, but he would not let the demons speak because they knew who he was.

Very early in the morning, while it was still dark, Jesus got up, left the house and went off to a solitary place, where he prayed. Simon and his companions went to look for him, and when they found him, they exclaimed: 'Everyone is looking for you!' Jesus replied, 'Let us go some-where else—to the nearby villages—so I can preach there also. That is why I have come.' So he travelled throughout Galilee, preaching in their synagogues and driving out demons.

MARK 1:32–39

I read this passage whenever I'm feeling under pressure, pulled in several directions by numerous demands. Every time, I'm struck by how amazingly single-minded and focused Jesus was. He knew his priorities, kept to his plan, and was always serene and secure in the face of pressure. Consider what happened here at Capernaum and look at Jesus' dilemma. The 'whole town' had gathered and he'd been healing 'many' of them, and there was a wonderful openness to God's Spirit at that particular moment. Yet there were probably as many people there the next day who still needed healing and ministry. In fact, when Simon came looking for him and found him on his own, you can almost hear the note of reproach in his voice: 'Everyone is looking for you!' In other words, 'What are you doing here on your own when all those people still need healing?' Imagine the moral pressure on Jesus. Surely it's not fair to heal half the village and leave the other half sick and disabled? But Jesus was absolutely clear about his priorities. He'd spent time with his Father in prayer and knew exactly what he had to do next. Very confidently he said, 'Let us go somewhere else—to the nearby villages—so I can preach there also. That is why I have come.'

In my experience, that would have been pastoral suicide! I imagine the Simon Peter types in my church might have replied, 'A lot of people are going to feel let down here, and, even though I understand, I'm not sure they will. But if you want to preach, you go ahead and do what you want to do.' By then, I would have felt crippled by guilt and backed into a corner. Jesus, however, had prayed out his priorities, organized his life and planned his strategy. He knew that he had to keep preaching and moving towards Jerusalem, because his ultimate vision involved a cross, and with it a far greater healing for the whole human race. That is why the rest of Mark's Gospel is full of movement and direction: 'Jesus left there'; 'Jesus withdrew'; 'Jesus went on... went up... went across... went around... came to another place'. And that is why we have to be very clear about our own direction, because the same Spirit will want to lead us toward another goal and another change, which takes us another step toward God's greater vision for our lives and for our church.

The problem for the average pastor, of course, is that instead of heading for Jerusalem with a vision, he or she is often left drowning in Capernaum, paralysed by a thousand different demands and the inability even to think clearly, never mind make plans. This can easily become the excuse for failing to make plans and prioritize, and ultimately the main reason why things will never change. Meanwhile, at the other extreme, there are leaders who use 'vision' as a kind of tonic to be taken liberally whenever they're feeling trapped or weary. If only for a moment, they love to talk about anything that will help them forget the painful realities of where they really are.

Unless the two extremes of constant talking and chronic inertia turn into some serious planning and implementing, however, the sense of weakness, failure and overall paralysis only increases. How, then, do we get the balance between dreaming and doing, vision and reality, thinking and task? What should we aim for and aspire to?

IMPOSSIBLE, DIFFICULT, DONE!

James Hudson Taylor (1832–1905) used to say that 'there are three stages in the work for God: Impossible; Difficult; Done.' Over the years, this has not only become my main slogan for change but has provided a helpful tool for going about it. Very simply, I've translated the stages of 'impossible, difficult, done' into the idea of dreams, visions and goals.

Dreams: out of our mind, 'impossible'

Most of us have a little 'dream box' in our brains that we mainly keep to ourselves and rarely open up to others. It's a pleasant thing to have, because it expresses who we are and where we'd like to be. Nevertheless, the contents are generally labelled 'impossible'. In fact, the Oxford English Dictionary defines the word 'dream' in four ways, two of which are potentially conflicting. A dream, it says, can be 'a cherished aspiration, ambition or ideal', and it can also be 'an unrealistic fantasy'. In God's economy, he specializes in taking the latter and turning it into reality.

The fulfilment of 'impossible' dreams has long been a significant part of God's dealings with his people. As an ageing, childless Abraham sat in the desert watching millions of stars, he heard the words, 'So shall your offspring be' (Genesis 15:5) and went on to follow an impossible dream of becoming 'a great nation' (12:2). Joseph had more than one impossible dream that ultimately led to his leadership of 'the whole land of Egypt' (41:41). Moses was given a dream of deliverance from that land against all possible odds (Exodus 3:7–12).

The dreaming continued throughout the Old Testament and into the New, when the dawning of the Church came with the impossible dream of turning a small 'upper room' congregation into a movement that would reach the ends of the earth (Acts 1:8). As it did so, God raised up more and more leaders with impossible dreams. When the missionary Hudson Taylor left for China, one of his colleagues told him, 'You are making a great mistake… You will be forgotten and the Mission won't live for seven years.' How many of us would have laid down the dream there and then? Taylor, however, saw many thousands come to faith and hundreds of missionaries embrace his dream. When, on one occasion, he made an appeal for 1000 workers, 1153 responded.[1]

In almost every case, God has chosen to use weak and ordinary human beings to accomplish extraordinary things. William Wilberforce not only struggled for 18 years to see his dream of abolishing slavery fulfilled, but he also had huge struggles with his health. Whenever he rose to speak in Parliament, many would smirk at the sight of what they described as a 'little ailing creature'. Even so, people would still crowd the benches to listen to his appeals, not least because the power of his dream gave him a passion and authority in delivering it, and, as the saying goes, 'turned the minnow into a whale'.

Some years ago, as a singer-songwriter, I used to see the same pattern repeated when I was privileged to sing and lead worship alongside some dynamic and world-changing leaders, from David Watson to Billy Graham. In every case you would meet the man and see his 'feet of clay', but the dream he carried would always explode with authority and passion whenever he spoke or acted in public. I worked with David Watson for five years, and saw the depressive and vulnerable side that he describes so honestly and movingly in his own writings. Like Wilberforce, he struggled with his health and his inner demons, but absolutely nothing ever dampened his dream of renewal and reconciliation within the Church. Over 15 years, his ministry in a half-empty church building in York turned into a ministry to thousands in cathedrals and city halls around the world.

What happened in all these cases was that an 'impossible' dream evolved over time into a 'difficult' vision, which was then broken down into some very achievable goals. Twenty years ago, my own little 'dream box' contained what then seemed a very naive aspiration to build a church of 1000 ordinary people, living in an ordinary area, who could also be a resource and encouragement to other churches. Based on my experience in York, it was a simple dream that seemed impossible to attain but inspirational enough to motivate and encourage me. Slowly but surely, the dream turned into a realistic vision, which became a definite goal, and I believe that this principle holds good for anyone who'll embrace it.

The dream doesn't have to involve a whole country, or abolition of some kind of evil on a global scale, or even a church of a thousand. What it does need, however, is a recognition that dreams are from God and are not sent to taunt and discourage us. Such dreams are God's gift to us all, not to the chosen few, so it's important that we learn, as the body of Christ, to dream together and pool our aspirations and hopes. In the next chapter, we'll see what that means in practice. Meanwhile, it's interesting to note that nearly 40 per cent of us dream constantly about a better future, even though that future is still beyond the horizon. Imagine the impact if every Christian were to offer their dreams to God, cultivating the eye of faith, not only to look forward but to focus on God's purposes.

Visions: out of the boat, 'difficult'

Dear God,
I have been reading all the things that happened long ago, when the sun stood still and David and Goliath and Daniel with the lions' den and the fall of Jericho. A lot of things happened in your day.
Yours truly, Joe[2]

If our dreams are not to remain unrealized, then it's important that we carry them through to the next stage. Otherwise, like that child's letter, we imply that the God of the Bible is no longer the one we believe in today. A dream evolves into a vision when we begin to work out what is practically possible today, in the here and now, and in our present predicament. I use the word 'predicament' because it implies something that is difficult and still beyond us, and a vision is exactly that. It is a difficult step forward into the future, and for that reason it is avoided by many. It stretches and tests our faith, as well as our commitment to move and grow. In other words, it requires that, like Peter in Matthew 14:29, we step out of our 'boat' towards Jesus, despite our doubts and fears and lack of confidence.

Boats appear in the Bible on several occasions, and the episodes involving them show us that when God gives a vision and calls us to follow, we can either step out of the boat, fall out, or be thrown out. Whichever is our experience, it is never entirely comfortable but is always of God, and essential in engaging with change.

The wake-up call

Hardest of all is being thrown out of the boat, but this is what happened to the reluctant prophet Jonah. Called to Nineveh, he set sail in a different direction and found himself in a raging storm at sea. Despite his desperate circumstances, he was sleeping below deck until woken by the news that the boat was sinking. In some ways, we could see the Church in a similar position, surrounded by storms that threaten its security and very existence but hoping that, if it goes to sleep and tries to forget the problems, the situation will somehow improve. It is, in fact, the sleep of despondency, depression and denial that so many suffer from today.

God's answer to Jonah was not only a wake-up call but a deliberate shake-up as he was picked up and thrown overboard into the very heart of the storm. Only then, as he started to be honest about his predicament, did he begin the process that eventually led to the embracing of a vision for salvation for Nineveh. To Jonah's credit, it was his own request to be thrown overboard, as he began to acknowledge his own denial and disobedience.

In the same way, the shaping of vision in a church is often preceded by a waking and shaking. Sometimes we really do need to wake up to the reality of our predicament. For a start, we should remember that any church, however large, is potentially only a generation away from extinction. We also need to reflect on the Church's falling attendances and stop making excuses for them. We need to recognize that many churches no longer have any children or youth in their congregations, and that 40 per cent of the UK population has never had any contact with the Church whatsoever. And we particularly need to be honest about the fact that more and more of our churches are becoming less and less financially viable. Difficult as it may be, it is honesty alone that leads to a humility that unlocks a hunger for change. As soon as we are honest, the sky begins to clear, our vision focuses and we begin to identify with Jonah as he starts to repent and embrace a more difficult but God-centred path: 'I have been banished from your sight; yet I will look again towards your holy temple' (Jonah 2:4).

The pride before the fall

At the other end of the spectrum, Simon Peter had the opposite problem to Jonah's. Far from retreating, he usually took the lead in going over the top and overboard. Unlike Jonah, he was wide open to change but also impulsive and overconfident. A single glance at Jesus walking on water and he was out of the boat, ready to copy his Master (Matthew 14:28–31). The problem was that the very waves that attracted him to try the miraculous threatened to drag him down into the depths of the lake. Essentially, his eyes were on the waves instead of on Jesus, on the miraculous possibilities instead of his God.

Many of us fall at the first hurdle of vision because we are swept away by waves of excitement at the prospect of doing something memorable and new. Peter had to learn what it meant to wait on God in the upper room, praying for the right moment and motive before he took on the world (see Acts 1). Similarly, we have to realize that going in our own strength can be just as debilitating as refusing God's strength; if we ignore this fact, we begin to sink and the vision is in danger of being lost.

Obeying the call

Peter and the disciples had another 'out of the boat' experience after the resurrection. It begins in John 21 with their rather despondent determination to get on with life after Jesus appears to have left them. They sat in their boat and proceeded to do the one thing that they knew they were good at—fishing—and they quickly discovered that they couldn't even do that. Sometimes we act in the same way. Whenever our vision of Jesus dims, we naturally turn back to our own human abilities and talents and our time-honoured ways of coping. Quite simply, we lose the vision and lose the plot.

When Jesus appeared to the disciples, standing on the lake shore, he began by asking a provocative question: 'Haven't you any fish?' 'No,' they had to reply. Like the disciples, we have to admit that without Jesus' presence and vision in our lives, even our professional talents and resources can amount to nothing. But then comes a simple command: '"Throw your net on the right side of the boat and you will find some." When they did, they were unable to haul the net in because of the large number of fish. Then the disciple whom Jesus loved said to Peter, "It is the Lord!"' (vv. 6–7).

Jesus' solution was refreshingly simple: 'Don't fish there; fish here. Don't do it that way; do it this way, my way.' Vision for the Christian is not actually a complex process. It may be difficult and painful to receive, but it was never designed by God to be incomprehensible without a PhD. Jesus' emphasis is never on 'fathom it out' but rather on 'follow me', and following in the end is more about faith and trust than fancy techniques. Standing on the shore, Jesus could see the shoals of fish that the disciples could not hope to see from the boat, and what to them seemed impossibly 'difficult' was only a single action away from being 'done'. All they had to do was listen and respond—to step out in faith. And that's when the third stage of setting a few simple goals kicks in.

Goals: out of the rut, 'done'

Whenever I think of goals, I prefer to think of football rather than management. In management, you can deploy a thousand different methods for setting and reaching goals. In football, you simply score them, one at a time, and celebrate each one in the making. That's how I've learnt to apply and implement vision. Yes, it's important to dream and then to step out of the boat and out of our depth, keeping our eyes fixed on Jesus. But what makes it achievable is moving forward, one step at a time. I love the old Chinese proverbs that say, 'A journey of a thousand miles begins with a single step' and 'Be not afraid of going slowly; be only afraid of standing still'.

Peter had definitely learnt to go more slowly by the time Jesus returned after the resurrection. This time, he didn't try to reach Jesus by walking on water, but simply 'jumped into the water' (John 21:7). Amazingly, that is all we have to do to follow our dream: jump in with a single leap, and be ready for the next move after that. The genius of Jesus' approach is that he never overwhelmed people with all the details all at once. As he left Capernaum, his initial goal was simply the nearby villages. Little by little, the vision was unfolding, but even as it did so, the disciples didn't really understand what was happening. Those of us who lead change need to take this on board. We will look at the role of leadership in later chapters; for now, the lesson is the importance of encouraging people to embrace dreams and engage with visions, but at the same time to focus on scoring goals, taking the next small step and getting something done. Once that happens, our faith begins to grow and we're ready for the step that follows.

To use another image, this is the 'seed' principle that Jesus loved to teach about. It can be applied in different ways, but it's particularly inspirational when we reflect on it in relation to the process of change: 'The kingdom of heaven is like a mustard seed, which a man took and planted in his field. Though it is the smallest of all your seeds, yet when it grows, it is the largest of garden plants and becomes a tree, so that the birds of the air come and perch in its branches' (Matthew 13:31–32).

UNTANGLING THE BRANCHES

Among those reading this book will be leaders with churches at very different stages of development. Some of us are nurturing very young plants and others are wondering whether their large tree can hold any more birds. As churches change and grow, it can be tempting to look for complex answers to what seem like increasingly complicated problems, and there is no shortage of books and resources, Christian and secular, to cater for this demand. If the gospel is good news for all, where and how it is communicated needs to be equally clear, simple and accessible, and not just for leaders of megachurches. Instead, however, most of us suffer from 'idea overload'. We not only end up with more and more books on our shelves and conferences in our diaries, but over seven million new pages are added to the worldwide web every day, while 60 billion pieces of junk mail are sent out every year.

Jesus worked very differently. Not only did he refuse to be tied in knots by the religious thinkers and leaders of his day but, when it came to changing people's thinking, he kept his teaching profoundly simple and used the image of a child to make the point: 'I tell you the truth, unless you change and become like little children, you will never enter the kingdom of heaven' (Matthew 18:3). Elsewhere, he prayed, 'I praise you, Father, Lord of heaven and earth, because you have hidden these things from the wise and learned, and revealed them to little children. Yes, Father, for this was your good pleasure' (Luke 10:21). The appeal here is to keep things simple, clear and completely focused. That is not to say that we stop communicating new ideas (or I wouldn't be writing this book), but that we should strive for a kind of childlike simplicity of approach that can easily and effectively be passed on to others.

Don Everts captures this focus beautifully in his book *Jesus with Dirty Feet*:

Jesus was not a Christian,
He never asked anyone to become a Christian,
    never built a steepled building,
    never drew up a theological treatise,
    never took an offering,
    never wore religious garments,
    never incorporated for tax purposes.
He simply called people to follow him.
That's it.
That, despite its simplicity, is it.
He called people to follow him…
It is never more
    than Jesus' call: 'Follow me'
    and a response: dropping familiar nets
    and following, in faith,
    this sandalled Jewish man.
It is never more than that.
Two thousand years of words can do nothing
to the simple, basic reality of Christianity:
Those first steps
    taken by those two brothers.
    Peter and Andrew's theology
    was as pure as it gets:
Jesus said, 'Follow me.' And we did.[3]

Of course, a combination of simple and profound is far from easy, and it can be challenging to produce a simple and inspiring vision of change that the whole church can own. Identifying the different stages of 'dreams, visions and goals' has helped me to make a start in planning change, but we need to go a little further in establishing a clear, firm basis for the whole process.

As somebody once put it, 'a mist in the pulpit is a fog in the pew', and that image is particularly apt in illustrating the importance of a clear vision. Imagine what happens when you're driving along the road and suddenly encounter a blanket of fog. You slow down, change gear, drive more hesitantly and generally feel far less comfortable and confident on the road. If the fog persists, you end the journey feeling weary and stressed—assuming you haven't taken a wrong turn and ended up in the wrong place. In the same way, a church that doesn't have a clear vision will move slowly and nervously, growing increasingly anxious at any sign of increasing speed. As time passes, the minister will lament the lost years and the wrong turnings, bewildered at where the church has ended up. Real-life fog can be a killer, but the fog of unclear vision can slowly kill the soul.

CLEARING THE FOG AND FINDING THE MAP

Navigating change can appear daunting and even dangerous for the novice, but it needn't be the case. As already mentioned, there are many models of management and change around, and many definitions of the key words 'vision', 'values', 'mission' and 'purpose'. The model I want to use here deliberately sets out to provide a simple map for change and to integrate the most commonly used words into a clear set of directions.

A map for change

This model is described by the author and management educator Jim Collins in his book *Beyond Entrepreneurship*.[4] In it, he uses a framework for defining vision that came out of extensive research from Stanford University, California, trying to address the common complaint that people find it hard to define what vision actually is.[5] All agree that it has 'a good feel' to it and is essential to great leadership, but what does it look like and where does it lead in practical terms?

A glance at the diagram shows that any vision has three basic components—values, purpose and mission—which form its essence. Once these components are in place, we can move on to formulate a practical strategy, setting out a range of specific tasks to accomplish the vision. Let's look briefly at each component in turn.

VALUES

Values are where vision begins. They have been described as the 'ether that permeates an organization—its decisions, its policies, its actions'.[6] When I wrote *The Challenge of Cell Church*, the whole thrust of the book (and its subtitle) was 'Getting to grips with cell church values'. For me, this was the single most important lesson that came out of the cell church movement, that vision never begins with the changing of structures but always with an examination of our values. The leading cell church consultant Bill Beckham used to drive the message home with this statement: 'Never change a structure, unless you change the value first. Otherwise the cost is always too high.'

Why is it so important to focus on our values before anything else? For the simple reason that whatever we value will always drive and motivate everything we do; hence the saying 'we do what we value, and value what we do'. We must never be tempted to think it's our visionary plan that drives us, however inspiring. The plan will keep us focused but essentially we are values-driven, so it's imperative that we recognize what actually drives us before we attempt to change anything.

Imagine, for instance, that you want to introduce an all-age service to attract young families to your church. The congregation may agree that it's a good plan and a viable strategy for growing the next generation of worshippers. If, however, what this congregation really values is formality, tradition and quiet reflection, then people will start to complain vociferously once the change has taken place. The fact that it previously seemed a sensible idea will now be irrelevant, because the church's true values have now been threatened or even completely removed. What has to happen is a prolonged learning process preceding the change, in which the values of informality, inclusion and cultural relevance are introduced and begin to be accepted. Only then will the change itself be fully successful. Moreover, we should note that it has been said that it can take at least five years for a church to change its values significantly.

At the heart of this issue is the fact that we need to recognize that our true values are not necessarily what we say they are, but what we demonstrate by our actual behaviour. This can result in a real minefield in terms of change, so those of us who are leaders need to preach and teach both sensitively and systematically in this whole area. Every major phase of change at St Mark's has been accompanied by a refocusing on our values. In the area of relationships, for instance, we have revisited the importance of unity, understanding, communication and conflict resolving; sermon series have ranged from 'Let us love one another' (studying all the 'one another' verses in the New Testament) to 'Watch your mouth!' (a series on the way we communicate). Looking back, I don't think we would ever have moved so far forward without this continuous and strategic focus on values.

In this whole process, we need to make two clear distinctions. First of all, as I've already suggested, we need to distinguish between our actual values and those we aspire to, but to help us do this we should also distinguish between our core values and our distinctive values. Our core values can simply be a list of bullet points that summarize what drives us and defines us as a church. A summary of the core values of the cell church movement is as follows:

- **All involved**: every member in ministry
- **Becoming disciples**: radically applying God's word to our lives
- **Creating community**: not just attending meetings, but sharing lives and building relationships
- **Doing evangelism**: as opposed to just talking about it
- **Encountering God**: expecting a release of his presence and power among his people.[7]

Notice how these values are set out in a simple ABCDE format to make them memorable for a congregation. While they can be expressed in very different ways, it's interesting that most growing churches and Christian movements tend to come up with some version of these same five values. It can be tempting to generalize, however, and allow our list of core values to be vague enough to be open to any interpretation, and for this reason it's healthy and helpful to go on to define our distinctive values. By this, I mean a more detailed list that describes what we mean in very practical terms. For instance, what might we emphasize in valuing discipleship? My own church would define it in the following way (see Appendix One for a full list of the distinctive values of St Mark's Church).

Becoming disciples

- from the cradle to the grave
- focused on Jesus
- centred on biblical revelation
- applied practically and personally
- bearing more and more fruit

We value:

- learning for the whole of life
- teaching that is systematic and inspirational
- application that enables response
- mentoring that is focused and full of encouragement
- training that is relevant, practical and varied

We value:

- the enquiring mind
- the open heart
- the passionate spirit
- seeking God in all things

Once a list like this has been agreed, every suggestion and decision for change can be measured alongside our distinctive values. Over time, this list is gradually transferred from the page to the heart, and to the memories and instincts of a whole congregation.

PURPOSE

Whenever I've been to a conference, read a book or digested the latest vision for change, I've always processed it with the conviction that churches are not meant to be clones, and that God puts his unique stamp on every situation. Every church is made up of many ingredients, ranging from each of its members to its cultural and community context, as well as its history. It's the sum of all those ingredients that gives us our unique DNA and, with it, our particular purpose. A purpose or mission statement, whether in business or the Church, describes very simply why the organization exists, setting out in a sentence or two how it wants to make its impact on the world. Jim Collins writes, 'A good purpose statement is broad, fundamental, inspirational, and enduring. It should serve to guide your organization for at least a hundred years.'[8]

As an example, my own church has a T-shirt and letterhead slogan ('pioneering a new future') which expands into our purpose statement: 'to pioneer a new future for the Church and its mission'. St Mark's began as a pioneer church plant nearly 100 years ago, and there is now a pioneering spirit at the very heart of the church, which not only allows it to embrace the challenge of change but also affects everything it does. Other churches, in city centres, for instance, become beacons for teaching the faith or ministering to the homeless or modelling multi-ethnic community. Churches near universities may specialize in ministering to students, or some parish churches may connect particularly with their local school or community groups, or rural churches may locate themselves at the very hub of village life. Wherever we are, our purpose statement should reflect and express what we do well and are well placed to do. That in itself is important, because too many of us attempt to do too many things without discerning where we're most obviously called and what we're most likely to accomplish. As a church, we need to know our main purpose, then learn to communicate it, celebrate it and capitalize on it in every change we make.

MISSION

If defining purpose is about the broad and bigger picture, mission is about having 'a clear and compelling overall goal'[9] to help achieve that purpose. Jim Collins explains it in the following way:

Unlike purpose, which is never achieved, a mission should be achievable. It translates values and purpose into an energizing, highly focused goal—like the moon mission. It is crisp, clear, bold, exhilarating. It reaches out and grabs people in the gut. It requires little or no explanation; people 'get it' right away.[10]

A phrase that has now been coined universally and expresses the essence of a good mission is BHAGS: big, hairy, audacious goals! Here are one or two examples from my own journey.

- The reordering of a church building in the context of spiritual renewal.
- The planting of a new church.
- The transition of a church to a cell-based model.
- The creation of a missional network of churches that are collaborating in new ways of doing church.

You will notice that none of these goals is achievable overnight. In fact, each one could be described as an 'out of the boat', difficult but doable vision. In the same way, your church may take on a mission to renew, reorder, restructure, resource or reinvent itself in some way. It will be an 'out of the boat' project and may take several years to complete, but it will take you beyond where you are now and equip and inspire the church to accomplish more of its overall calling. All you need to do is to step out of the boat in defining it, and make sure that it flows directly from your core values and your overriding purpose.

STRATEGY AND TASKS

Once we have embarked on a specific mission, we then need to break it down into clear, simple and realistic steps. Essentially a strategy answers the question, 'How will we achieve our mission?' Best management practice suggests that a strategy should have no more than five or six clear goals to accomplish. A building project, for instance, may define its strategy under the headings of vision, design, finance and delivery. Each of those areas will then be broken down into simple action steps that answer the question, 'What is to be done, by whom, by when, and by what means?' I have also found the SMART model very helpful in planning and thinking about practical goals. Very simply, it states that our goals should always be

- **S**pecific
- **M**easurable
- **A**chievable
- **R**ealistic
- **T**imed

In other words, let's keep it simple, but let's be focused, organized and strategic in everything we aim to do.

SHAPING UP

There is far more material available on vision planning, but I want the emphasis here to be on inspiration rather than information.

While some people are more inclined to engage with detailed and analytical approaches to management, others prefer a more fluid approach. All of us, though, can look to Jesus and learn from him. As we do, he will challenge but never overwhelm us. Remembering our Gospel passage at the start of this chapter, we can be sure that Jesus understands only too well the kind of pressures that Capernaum can bring, with its conflicting and competing demands and the clamour of the crowd for attention. Instead, however, he offers us a call to prayer and a different kind of pressure, one that challenges us to focus more on Jerusalem, with its greater vision and strategic mission, and one that speaks to us clearly about priorities. After that, he simply asks that we step out of the boat, one step at a time, and obey the call to 'follow me'.

———— ✦ ————

MEETING THE CHALLENGE

Dreams

- Does your church have a dream?
- What are your dreams for your church?

Visions

- What is your church doing at the moment that could be described as 'out of the boat' and difficult?

Goals

- Looking at the SMART model, how intentional is your church in setting clear goals?

Values

- Brainstorm a list of what you believe your church really values. Compare your lists, then compile a common list. Discuss and add to that list the values you would like to impart to the church.

Purpose

- What is the defining characteristic of your church that gives it direction and purpose?
- Complete the sentence: 'Our church exists to ....'

Mission

- What specifically does your church hope to achieve in the next five years?
- Does this mission flow directly out of its values and purpose?
- Does the whole church know and understand what its mission is?

Strategy and tasks

- Devise a strategy for your church over the next six to twelve months, to further its mission. Compile a list of SMART goals (no more than half a dozen), and then add a list of specific tasks under each goal to help you get there.

✜

Chapter Three

SHAPING PEOPLE:
THE PROCESS OF CHANGE

It has been said that, in the process of leading change, most of us overestimate what can be achieved in one year but tend to underestimate what can change over five years, and that is certainly an accurate assessment of my own experience in leading a church. The period between year one and year five, however, can be so fraught with obstacles and hurdles that not only can we begin to lose sight of our mission, but we can also start to lose any sense of progress and momentum.

The following alternative story of Noah has appeared in different guises over the years, usually under the title 'Noah's lament', and it offers an apt and amusing reminder that shaping people and processing change has never been an easy task.

And the Lord said unto Noah, 'Where is the ark which I have commanded thee to build?'

And Noah said unto the Lord, 'Verily, I have had three carpenters off ill. The gopher-wood supplier hath let me down—yea, even though the wood hath been on order for nigh upon twelve months. What can I do, Lord?'

And the Lord said unto Noah, 'I want that ark finished even after seven days and seven nights.' And Noah said, 'It will be so.'

And it was not so. And the Lord said unto Noah, 'What seemeth to be the trouble this time?' And Noah said unto the Lord, 'Mine subcontractor hath gone bankrupt. The pitch which thou commandest me to put on the outside and on the inside of the ark hath not arrived. The plumber hath gone on strike. Shem, my son who helpeth me on the ark side of the

business, hath formed a rock band with his brother Ham and Japheth.
Lord, I am undone.'

And the Lord grew angry and said, 'And what about the animals, the
male and the female of every sort that I ordered to come unto thee to keep
their seed alive upon the face of the earth?'

And Noah said, 'They have been delivered unto the wrong address but
should arriveth on Friday.'

And the Lord said, 'How about the unicorns and the fowls of the air by
sevens?' And Noah wrung his hands and wept, saying, 'Lord, unicorns are
a discontinued line; thou canst not get them for love nor money. And fowls
of the air are sold only in half dozens. Lord, Lord, thou knowest how it is.'

And the Lord in his wisdom said, 'Noah, my son, I do knowest. Why else
dost thou think I have caused a flood to descend upon the earth?'

I have to confess to loving this irreverent take on the story of Noah. It used to bring a smile to my face in the middle of building projects, and helped me to stop taking myself or my vision too seriously when the pressure was on. I've never had to go beyond the real scriptures, however, to find many authentic examples of the change process, with its rollercoaster ride of highs and lows. Abraham, Isaac and Joseph all provide food for thought and teaching as I read how they journeyed in faith and pursued their dreams, facing challenges and changes galore. As a church, we've looked at the book of Exodus, following Moses as he went through painful periods of personal change before leading God's people from slavery into a desert on the way to the promised land. We've been inspired by Joshua and what it means to cross over from the old to the new and to possess an ever-changing landscape, from the fortified cities to the streams of Gilead. We've also followed Nehemiah as he mourned the broken state of his people before embracing a vision for rebuilding and renewal.

In all these cases, the process of change was messy and unpredictable. No doubt the biggest reason for this, by far, was that it involved people—human beings who were fallible and frustrating, and often quite foolish. Not surprisingly, the Bible reflects far more on the relational issues in these stories than on the heroic and visionary accomplishments. Joseph's meteoric rise to fortune is all but eclipsed by the five and a half chapters dedicated to his reconciliation with his brothers and the healing and building of those family relationships. Similarly, the stories of Moses and Nehemiah are riddled with examples of people struggling with change—rebelling, grumbling and disagreeing, then getting on board or back on track, and braving the next move forward.

In this chapter I want to look at the processes that people inevitably go through in coping with change. As well as illustrating principles from the previous two chapters, we'll consider how these stages of handling change can be managed, especially in a local church context.

CONNECTION: GETTING SWITCHED ON

One of the most successful business books on change is a short and simple parable called *Who Moved My Cheese? An amazing way to deal with change in your work and your life*.[1] It is the story of two mice and two 'Littlepeople' who live in a maze and look for cheese to nourish them and make them happy. Cheese is, of course, a metaphor for what you are searching for in life, and the maze is where you look for it. The maze itself is full of dark corners, blind alleys and places to get lost, and yet there are also wonderful places, filled with cheese, to be found there. The mice, having 'simple brains and good instincts', simply run around without a care in the world, and discover room after room of cheese. The 'Littlepeople', on the other hand, have 'complex brains, filled with many beliefs and emotions'. (Remind you of any Christians you know?) Early on, they discover their first mountain of cheese, and their behaviour from then on looks uncannily like that of many church members.

First of all, they find that this particular supply of cheese offers them a sense of security, so they quickly decide to stop looking for it anywhere else. In fact, the cheese is in such abundance that they eventually decide to move next door, building a permanent home there. Over time, they become so comfortable in their routine that they fail to see that the cheese has gradually diminished and that they themselves are now living in denial, emotionally disconnected from the reality of their predicament. When the cheese eventually runs out, all they can do at first is to protest and cry, 'It's not fair.' Before very long, however, with no food to survive on, they become full of fear and denial, afraid of the maze, while still pining for the past. The rest of the parable follows their journey back into the maze and the lessons they learn about the challenge of change along the way.

Before a church can change, it needs to recognize that all its resources (the cheese) have to be searched for and, when found, have to be replenished. It needs to understand the consequences of staying in one place and refusing to move, and it has to overcome its anxieties about moving as well as its fear of change (travelling into the maze). Only then can it begin the necessary process of change. In spiritual terms, this means developing what many Christian writers have called a 'holy discontent', and the events of the Israelite exodus illustrate it well.

At the beginning of the story, the people were relatively settled, considering they were slaves. Even though a new and despotic Pharaoh had appeared on the scene, they still had employment and food and their own separate community social life, so they weren't motivated to change. Only when the order came to kill all the male Hebrew babies (Exodus 1:16, 22) did their attitude begin to change. Some time after that, God sent Moses to call them out of Egypt and into the desert, where they would be shaped into his special people. How, then, do we create an atmosphere of 'holy discontent', especially when a church appears secure and comfortable and not immediately threatened with decline or closure? How do we help the congregation have a more realistic picture of itself and also begin to shape a vision for the future?

Preaching, teaching and prayer

We have already hinted at the importance of preaching, teaching and prayer, but let's spell it out here in the context of provoking holy discontent. Moses encountered much discontent on his journey with the Israelites, but it was rarely holy. After the agony and anger surrounding the golden calf episode, he desperately appealed to God for a way forward, and prayed two important prayers in Exodus 33. He prayed, 'Teach me your ways' (v. 13) and 'Show me your glory' (v. 18), in effect appealing to know more of God's word and experience more of his Spirit. The two together, in equal measure, are essential for any change of heart, and yet churches often allow themselves to be weak on one or the other. In my experience, the saying is true:

All word and no Spirit, we dry up;
all Spirit and no word, we blow up;
word and Spirit together, we grow up.

In the famous Bayeux tapestry, there is an image of William the Conqueror prodding his soldiers from behind with a spear. When the words underneath were first translated into the English language, they read, 'William comforteth his soldiers'. This is precisely the kind of prodding 'comfort' that the Holy Spirit wants to give to our hearts, helping us to grow and change, and we ignore it at our peril. For this reason, the preachers among us need to be focused and intentional in applying God's word to where people actually are in the process of change, addressing the principles discussed in the previous two chapters in a way that brings both comfort and discomfort.

Equally, when we gather as a church for prayer, we apply the saying that 'prayer is not an easy way of getting what we want, but the only way of becoming what God wants us to be'. When we pray through the challenge of change, then, we not only need to ask God to inspire us with a holy discontent. We should also come with a 'Lord, will you show us?' approach, rather than 'Lord, will you bless it?' Often surrounded by conflicting opinions and convictions, it can be very reassuring for church members to see that the only convictions that will count in the end are the convictions given by the Holy Spirit, through his revelation as we wait on him.

Past, present and future

When we look for further clues in the scriptures as to how to connect people with the challenge of change, it's remarkable how often we find God reminding his people of their history. Very simply, he connects with them by retelling their story, applying the lessons of the past to the realities of the present, with the promise of blessing in the future in return for obedience. Over the years, I've discovered that linking past, present and future is a powerful tool in opening people to the possibilities of change. The past, in particular, has a powerful pull on people's hearts, for good or ill, and I've seen the importance of harnessing, honouring and healing the past as we aim to lead people into the future. The mistake we often make is to be so focused on the future that we ignore the past and assume it to be no longer relevant, when in fact the very opposite is the case.

The past can first of all be *harnessed*. A point of pride for St Mark's was that the church had been built in 1910 by its own congregation, in a poor mining community. In fact, there are many families who either remember or recount how their grandparents 'chipped the bricks', and how sacrificially people gave to see the church built. As a result, any suggestion of removing the pews and reordering their building was perceived by some as close to blasphemy. Undeniably, theirs had been an inspiring story of vision, commitment, faith and courage, with many of the values to match. What was important was not only to recognize that, but to retell and reflect on the story as a powerful example of what was needed in the present. Their predecessors had made huge sacrifices in order to give their grandchildren a future, so the challenge before the present church was clear: would they do the same for the generations to come? Would they reinvest in and renew the building that had been handed to them so generously, or would they risk doing nothing for their own children and children's children, eventually wear out the present resources, and have nothing to hand on? Acknowledging the story is a powerful way of connecting and motivating people, and this particular narrative could probably be repeated in a similar form in many other local churches today.

The second way we can connect with people is by ensuring that the past is *honoured*. One of the principles that our architect encouraged us to take on board was that, ideally, the design of our church buildings should have something of the past, present and future about it, reflecting the God who is 'the same yesterday and today and forever' (Hebrews 13:8). The benefit of reordering an older building (unless it is intrinsically ugly and falling apart) is that it can be redesigned to be functional in the present, and flexible and adaptable enough to make room for the future. At the same time, its more attractive historical features can be kept, restored and even enhanced, to remind the community of its journey so far.

'The journey so far' is important to remember in planning the journey ahead. It may well be right to transform the worship radically, for instance, but equally important to assess the impact on the congregation, especially if they have followed a particular pattern for the last 70 years or so. I arrived at St Mark's with many ideas about worship, but was also moved by the fact that significant numbers of older members had already seen their weekly Prayer Book service stripped back to only two a year. Before we introduced more radical changes to the contemporary worship service, we decided to reinstate the traditional service, as an additional option, on a monthly basis. This reflected the fact that we still had a significant number of worshippers who quite literally belonged to another era. It wasn't a case of challenging people to move with the times, because at 80 years (and counting), they had not only spent the best years of their life in an earlier time and culture, but had very little time left to go on worshipping in the way to which they had long been accustomed. The church needed to be both pastorally sensitive and culturally relevant to this sizeable and traditional elderly group. In this situation, it meant actually moving the service to the afternoon instead of early morning. The case for this was made by the senior members themselves, who preferred to gather in the middle of the day, after the early morning chill and before the failing light, and this smallest of practical changes, along with the hire of a 'pick up' bus, led to an enlarged congregation.

The challenge of change is not always about seeing into the future, but about relevance for all and about honouring the past, learning to bless it and build on it, and never just bludgeoning it out of existence. The result, in our case, was not only a happier congregation but an elderly group that was now prepared to bless all the other major changes in the church, knowing that they still had an honoured place at the heart of the worshipping community.

The past is a powerful ingredient to be harnessed and honoured, but it often needs to be *healed* as well. If past changes have been made hurtfully, clumsily or ill-advisedly, then their impact will haunt the present. Sometimes old wounds need to be healed through a careful listening and learning process, which then moves on purposefully to a renewed focus on the future.

CONCEPTION: DREAMING THE DREAMS

We have seen now that change never begins simply with a connection to a vision, but with the heart opening itself to fresh possibilities. Once that is happening, we can move with greater confidence to the next stage, where the vision itself is conceived and comes into being. By definition, conception is a delicate moment that needs a safe and secure environment, but it is also a life-giving and almost reckless moment that requires a creative atmosphere in order to thrive.

Those two words, 'delicate' and 'creative', must be held in tension as the vision is conceived. When I first arrived at St Mark's, I organized an away-day to develop our future vision and consider what kind of changes would need to take place. I knew I had to recognize the delicacy of the moment, as a young and visionary vicar coming in with a stream of new ideas. I had to be completely honest and transparent, and yet willing to be vulnerable and proved wrong. I knew also that major mistakes had been made in processing change in the past, so I began the away-day by saying, 'I want you to know that what you see is what you get, and you may be surprised or even shocked at some of my ideas for change, but you never need look beyond or beneath what is being said, because I will always be open, vulnerable and transparent with you, and I want you to be the same.' This approach created a breathing space where new ideas could be expressed and debated in an atmosphere of trust and transparency.

Once the mood of trust has been set, then the dreaming can begin. At this point, it is important to draw a distinction between dreams and visions. Dreams are usually deemed 'impossible' at this stage, and so they are not a serious and direct threat to the status quo. As a result, they appear both harmless and hopeless to opposers of change, while opening the door of vision to those who are desperate for it. Either way, the expression of dreams unites people around a common desire for a better future. To help this process, the following questions might be asked:

- What kind of a church would you like to hand on to your children and grandchildren?
- What would the ministry, the worship and the building look like?
- If you are involved in a particular ministry (for example, children and youth), what resources does it need to make it more effective and enable growth?
- What other ministries do we want to offer to people but cannot because we lack the resources?
- How could our buildings be improved for welcome, worship and further ministry?

- How can our church have a strong and healthy relationship with our surrounding community?

At this initial 'just dreaming' stage, negative questions should be banned—and especially questions about finance. If money is made the main focus from the beginning, most visionary projects will fizzle out quickly, because they will inevitably cost far more than is available at present. The secret is to keep thinking in terms of those three stages of God's work—'impossible, difficult, done'—and to keep on valuing and encouraging people's dreams. The church and business consultant David Cormack used to quote the saying, 'Do not fear those who dream while they sleep. It's those who dream when they're awake who mean business.' A church congregation begins to wake up and mean business when it learns to start dreaming.

CONSTRUCTION: BUILDING THE VISION

Assuming that hearts are beginning to open and dreams are emerging, it is time to identify some building blocks on which to base the vision as it emerges. At this stage, generating movement and momentum is crucial. Too many church leaders end up like the vicar who used to be seen watching the local train go by, every day at midday. When asked why he did this, he replied, 'It's the only thing in the parish that moves without me having to push it!' So how do we go about creating movement and momentum? Here are some ideas.

- **Entry points:** Often, we can discover natural God-given opportunities to put change on the agenda. If the organ has broken, the choir master has died, the hymn books are tattered, the church is full, the chapel is empty, the roof is leaking, or the buses aren't running, any one of these issues can provide an entry point for discussing the bigger issues about where the life of the congregation is going. Identifying natural entry points can accelerate the process of change and prove the proverb that 'the beginning is the half of every action'.

- **Easy steps:** I have said it already, but it is vital to keep dreams big and goals small. If people are nervous about change, they need to see that it is achievable in stages, and they also need to see early success. Easy steps meet this need.
- **Knock-on effects:** Each and every short-term win sends a positive message that change is a beneficial process and the vision is on track. Success breeds confidence, which is partly why most churches that have engaged in a visionary building project see an immediate surge in the effectiveness of their overall ministry soon afterwards, along with a desire for further vision and change. Look for the knock-on effects and capitalize on them.
- **'Knock-out' stories:** Good news is not only encouraging but energizing. It begins with hearing other people's stories, seeing the fruit of their labour, and embracing all the possibilities that their experiences open up. But it becomes an even more powerful motivator once we generate it from within. That is why every piece of good news and evidence of success should be celebrated and shared along the way, telling the story as it happens and affirming progress so far.
- **Knock-backs:** No church is immune from the 'Noah' syndrome, and things will inevitably go wrong. The important thing is to anticipate this, to prepare ourselves for it, and then to process events in a positive way. Learning how to be constructive in adversity is an important part of the change process overall.

CONSIDERATION: INCLUDING EVERYONE

Any church that is navigating change has to consider where different people are in terms of accepting the process. A well-known study by Roger and Shoemaker shows how people accept change at different rates.[2] They identified five groups of people, represented proportionally on the bell curve.

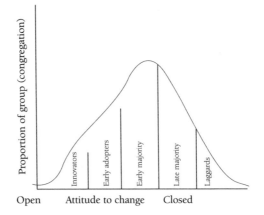

'Innovators' and 'laggards' represent the two extremes—those who promote any kind of change and those who oppose every change. The danger is allowing either of these groups to be the most vocal, as they will almost certainly misrepresent the majority. The interaction between the middle three groups is always crucial in bringing people on board. The 'early adopters' will influence the 'early majority' until a tipping point is reached, when the 'late majority' will decide to follow what has clearly become an overall majority.

Meanwhile, it is important to identify opinion leaders across the groups, who can become the main energizers for change. In a fascinating book called *The Tipping Point*,[3] Malcolm Gladwell looks at major changes that have occurred across society and throughout history, and shows how the combination and build-up of 'little things' can create a tipping point for sudden and rapid change. Of three main factors that he discusses, the first one focuses on the role that people play, and three kinds of people in particular—connectors, communicators and convincers.

Connectors (of people)

These are the natural networkers who connect different groups and factions together. In our context, this person could be a church warden whose whole family belongs to the church, from the children who go to the Sunday school to the elderly parent who attends the lunch club and the traditional Eucharist. Meanwhile, the warden herself is involved in the music, attends a home group and visits the sick. It goes without saying that one well-connected person of this kind will be a natural opinion leader in any process of change, connecting lots of very different people while sharing the same message.

Communicators (of information)

These people are not necessarily preachers, but they are gifted translators of information who take hold of a vision or idea and make it more accessible to particular groups. Whatever the vision, it will need communicating in very different ways to, say, teenagers, senior members and men on the fringe of the church. On many occasions, I have shared a particular idea or vision with my children, or an elderly church member, or a total outsider, and their response has been, 'So what you really mean is…'. They have then proceeded to restate and repackage my whole vision in a completely different language. However gifted I may think I am at communicating, I need others to help me engage effectively and relevantly with the sheer variety of people that the average congregation contains.

Convincers (of ideas)

These are the 'salespeople' who can persuade even the most ardent objector. In fact, the most effective convincers are often the people who once opposed the vision but are now on board. Simply asking them to share their journey with others can help those who struggle with change to connect and process the vision they are being asked to accept.

Together, these three types of people have an enormous impact. They draw others in, and then they explain, galvanize and inspire. Occasionally, a church leader may be blessed with all three attributes, but he or she will still need a team of other opinion leaders to produce the tipping point. They may not be highly articulate or even intentionally strategic; what is important is that they are to be found somewhere in most communities, including the church. Needless to say, they should be identified, prayed for and deployed.

Of course, it would be very unhelpful to address people publicly as 'laggards' and 'late majorities', yet it is important to help people to see where they are in the whole process and affirm them in their position. During our first major building project, somebody very helpfully came up with the image of a train that was heading towards a new destination. What they pictured was an old type of train, with an engine at the front, pulling everybody along (the leaders of change), and a guard's van at the back, watching everyone else (the laggards). We regularly used this image and invited people to 'board the train' and embrace the vision, but we also emphasized that it would stop at many stations along the way. At every station (every gift day, every presentation and every stage of change), we made the invitation to 'board' again. The message was very clear: people come on board at different stages of the journey and from very different places, and it is right and appropriate to respect where they are in processing the vision.

This proved to be an inspirational picture, and without it there would have been a real danger of serious division. The problem with many major projects is that people can so easily get the impression that 'you are either for or against', and those who are not quite ready can feel pressurized into making a decision. People think and act and are motivated in very different ways, and it's essential to honour that while working to bring everyone on board.

Finally, we should also consider those who will never come with us. As a pastor, I've often reflected on people's temperament, situation or circumstance and realized that there will always be some who feel unable to follow, for whatever reason. There's a moving example of this in 2 Samuel 19, when King David was returning to Jerusalem and his followers were gathering to accompany him. Among them was Barzillai, who was 'a very old man, eighty years of age' (vv. 31–39). He had been a loyal and loving follower of David, but Jerusalem was a destination too far. In a moving passage, he and David bless each other and release each other to go their separate ways. That story has helped me understand the role of those who cannot come with us. Major change may often be a journey too far for the very elderly among us, for example, and yet they still have a vital role in offering us their blessing. There have been many times when I've felt grateful for a mutual sense of relief and release, as we've agreed that they shouldn't even try to move with us but can and will pray for us and bless us.

COMMUNICATION: REACHING EVERYONE

Benjamin Disraeli, a 19th-century British Prime Minister, is quoted as saying, 'Talk to a man about himself, and he will listen for hours.' When it comes to communicating vision and change successfully, the secret lies in conveying the message that 'this is all about you'. If change is challenging, a typical initial response is lack of ownership: 'This is not really relevant to me, so I won't bother to listen.' In that kind of climate, inviting people to a special gathering to hear the vision is not enough. It needs to be raised at every church gathering, and in a way that conveys its relevance to every group. Any major project, from reordering the building to reordering the worship, will affect the whole church in some way, so we need to put ourselves in the shoes of each and every member, think about how it will affect them, and then communicate that 'this is all about you'. This checklist of questions can help us prepare our approach.

- What is and what is not changing?
- Why are we making this change?
- What is the overall rationale and what will the result be?
- Who will benefit and how?
- How does it look from their point of view?
- What are the potential concerns, obstacles and objections?
- What do they already know, and what do they need to know?
- What do they need to see and hear?
- How will they be feeling?
- How do we want them to feel?

In all this, we need to bear in mind four aspects of communication. As the questions suggest, *information* is key. Not only must we communicate fully, anticipating questions, objections and doubts, but communication must be simple and clear. This may mean prioritizing the 'headlines' in the main presentation and then communicating the finer details by other means, either in the question time that follows or through one-to-one conversations, handouts, brochures, emails and letters. Any major vision brings with it many finer details that need to be communicated along the way. The secret is to communicate little and often, and to prioritize the important points at each stage. Variety in communication is also important, so the additional use of PowerPoint, DVD, personal testimony and team presentation are all helpful, as is constant repetition. Generally speaking, people have to hear a message many times before the penny of understanding really drops.

Inclusion is another vital aspect of communication. It's important in any organization to be mindful of interested parties, but in the body of Christ we go further and aim much higher as we try to apply the principles of 'no division' and 'equal concern'.

The eye cannot say to the hand, 'I don't need you!' And the head cannot say to the feet, 'I don't need you!' On the contrary, those parts of the body that seem to be weaker are indispensable, and the parts that we think are less honourable we treat with special honour… But God has combined the members of the body and has given greater honour to the parts that lacked it, so that there should be no division in the body, but that its parts should have equal concern for each other (1 Corinthians 12:21–25).

Inclusion, then, will mean going out of our way to communicate directly and enthusiastically to a wide and diverse selection of church groups, including home groups, ministry groups, activity groups and all other special interest groups, making the link with the issues that are particularly relevant and important to them.

Aiming for clarity, variety and inclusion will require us to use imagination, but the spark that will set people's hearts alight can only come from *inspiration*. People have to see that the church leaders believe in the changes both personally and passionately. The great 19th-century preacher and teacher C.H. Spurgeon used to tell his students that whenever they spoke about heaven to people, their whole face should light up and radiate the joy of the message. He then added that whenever they spoke about hell, their 'ordinary face would do'. Most significant changes are an extraordinary event in the life of a church, and those with the responsibility of communicating what's happening cannot afford to meet potentially hard-hearted listeners with half-hearted arguments and presentation. As Shakespeare wrote in *Hamlet*, 'Suit the action to the word, the word to the action' (Act III Scene 2).

Finally, all good communication needs *illustration*, especially when it comes to putting across vision. By definition, vision is about seeing things, but communicating a vision means asking people to see something that is still invisible. Somehow, we need to create an image of the future that not only brings the change into focus, but also presents it in an attractive way. Illustration takes many forms, but the use of images, metaphors and stories all help to convey a message. When we reordered our church building, people were naturally anxious about investing in something they couldn't actually see. At first, when we talked about chairs instead of pews, many could only imagine what they had observed in the nearby chapels, where the chairs were not only uncomfortable but ugly and unstable. We had to take them to beautifully reordered church buildings and invite them to sit on modern padded seats. And when we talked about knocking down walls and adding rooms with glass doors, and an enormous glass frontage on the church, many could not get beyond their images of the local supermarket. We ended up spending a significant amount of our initial budget on a full-colour brochure, as well as a scale model, and, although I was initially sceptical, this proved to be one of the more inspirational decisions of the project. Many people became excited and committed once they could actually set their eyes on the proposal and see it in 3D.

COLLABORATION: INVOLVING EVERYONE

Tell me and I'll forget.
Show me, and I may not remember.
Involve me, and I'll understand.
NATIVE AMERICAN PROVERB

Collaboration—getting people involved—is another vital ingredient in bringing about change. The emphasis here is on collaboration, not just cooperation. We can apply all the principles of communication and convince people that change is good and right and necessary, but understanding is not the same as ownership. Similarly, involvement is not the same as investment, and yet it's only as people get involved that they can take the vital decision to invest. This means that when we engage with the various groups in a church, we don't just communicate a vision and ask them to cooperate, but we invite them to collaborate, to share in the decisions and become part of the process.

For us at St Mark's, this meant that I would share a vision for major change with my leadership team, and together we would refine and improve it and remove some of my wackier ideas. It would then be shared with the wider leadership, including the church council, where it would be pruned, refined and extended further. After that, it would be shared with the small groups of every kind, and they would be invited to ask questions, share concerns and add any other ideas. By the time the vision was presented to the church as a whole, the degree of ownership and investment was already very high.

CONSENSUS AND COMPROMISE: INTEGRATING EVERYONE

It goes without saying that holding together the principles of unity and diversity are essential for the health of any church. But how do we maintain this when it comes to major decisions for change? First of all, *consensus* is important. A 60/40 vote is hardly going to promote unity and cohesion, however important the change. That is not to say that lack of consensus means loss of vision, but it is often an indicator that the timing is simply wrong and that the majority are not quite ready.

During our building project, we made many radical decisions, but the one that could have split the church was over whether or not to remove the pulpit. Many could see that it would become an eyesore if it remained, but just as many were attached to the idea that it represented the very foundations upon which the church was built, and was therefore immovable and non-negotiable. Seeing a strong division developing over the issue, we simply left the pulpit where it was, although it didn't look right in the newly designed space. Ten years later, we revisited the proposal, and the decision to remove the pulpit was instant, painless and unanimous. When consensus can't be found, either the vision is not yet clear or the values have not yet been embraced. Either way, it can be very important to wait, watch and pray—with one possible exception.

A few of us are called to lead tiny, unviable churches, populated by a diehard remnant who care nothing for the core values of the

Christian Church. For them, the fullness of life that Jesus wanted to impart to everyone (John 10:10) is all but eclipsed by a self-centred life that is solely focused on religious taste and the preservation of the status quo. In such cases, the God-given vision itself may be to build from scratch, facing down the opposition where necessary—although thankfully these cases are few and far between. Where they do exist and when we are called, it is important that we go with the backing, support and blessing of the wider Church and its leadership, and that we meet inevitable aggression with grace. It is also essential to pay attention to the consensus in our own hearts that tells us when it's right to engage in conflict and when we should walk away. Too many Christian leaders have nervous breakdowns or suffer from clinical depression as a result of misguided calls to brave the pain.

The other key word at this point is *compromise*, a word that doesn't go down well in Christian circles when we're talking about holiness. But in this context, when agreement is needed on minor issues, compromise is an important virtue, bringing about agreement and mutual submission. An example that still brings a smile to my face was the choice of our new church carpet. Our décor team had decided on two possible colours, blue and green, but could not agree on the final choice. When they brought the issue back to the church council, half the members wanted blue and the other half green. We then took it to the whole church, and again the verdict was half and half. So we went to the carpet company and asked them to design us a blue-green carpet. Visitors often comment on the attractive and very unusual blending of colour.

CHARACTER FORMATION: EMBRACING CHANGE

We would rather be ruined than changed. We would rather die in our dread than climb the cross of the moment and let our illusions die.
W.H. AUDEN

Running through a list of principles and illustrations of change may send the message that it is easily and quickly achieved, but I know from painful experience that this is not the case. I also know how painful the process can be, from walking (and sometimes weeping) alongside broken colleagues who couldn't face the challenge any more. Again, from experience I know that there are two kinds of brokenness at this point. Faced with the challenge of change, there are leaders who are poor in spirit, embracing their own weakness and open to the pain of change, and those who have pulled out in spirit, refusing to face the challenge and count the cost. In extreme cases, you can watch a whole church choose to die in its dread, acutely aware of its desperate need to change but dreading the challenge of it even more.

W.H. Auden's image of consciously climbing on to a cross is powerfully apt. Significant change is always an uphill climb, and certainly seems at times to lead only to crucifixion and death. The novelist Amelia Barr (1831–1919) summed it up when she wrote, 'All changes are more or less tinged with melancholy, for what we are leaving behind is part of ourselves.' While this is true, the hope of the gospel message is that the cross is only the end of the beginning, and that resurrection and new life are really where we are heading when we follow God's way.

As our own church closed for reordering and we nervously left the building for twelve months, we were led out by an enormous model caterpillar, carried by scores of our children who hid underneath its coat. A year later, the same caterpillar led the procession into the new building, and then the children pulled away the caterpillar's coat and emerged to run through the church dressed in butterfly costumes. There was hardly a dry eye as people shared the joy of the moment and reflected on some of the pain of their journey. It reminds me of the cartoon of two caterpillars watching a butterfly gliding overhead: one says to the other, 'You'll never catch me going up in one of those'! At the outset, change can seem not only distant and strange, but way beyond our aspirations and abilities. To face it, we have to face down our 'dread', step out in faith and then follow the way of the cross. As American novelist James Baldwin put it, 'Not everything that is faced can be changed, but nothing can be changed until it is faced.'

There is one final point to make about process: it never ends. In God's economy and in an ever-changing world, 'constant change is here to stay'. The completion of one change is like the changeover stage in a relay race. To win the race, we must keep passing the baton, totally focused on enabling the next phase of the race to begin. And when eventually we reach the finishing line, no doubt we'll reflect on the process and agree with the sentiment expressed by Frances Hodgson Burnett in the children's book *The Secret Garden*: 'At first, people refuse to believe that a strange new thing can be done, then they begin to hope that it can be done, then they see that it can be done—then it is done and all the world wonders why it was not done centuries ago.'[4]

---- ✢ ----

MEETING THE CHALLENGE

Connection

- Is there a 'holy discontent' in your church at the moment? What is it?
- What is your personal holy discontent?
- What parts of your church's past need to be harnessed, honoured or healed?

Conception

- Go through the 'just dreaming' questions under this heading, and develop a common dream.

Construction

- Where are the entry points for opening up a discussion on change?
- If you have a current project involving change, has it been broken down into easy steps? What are they?
- Where can you aim at creating a knock-on effect from something good that has recently happened in the life of your church?
- Have you any knock-out stories to share with the church at the moment? Where and when can they be told?
- How do you handle the inevitable knock-backs that come your way? Do you address them constructively through the worship, teaching, prayer life and fellowship in your church?

Consideration

- How would you consider your church handles change? Does it oppose, resist, accept, welcome, encourage, or demand it?
- Who are the opinion leaders in your church?
- Who are the connectors, communicators and convincers, and how are they being deployed?

Communication

- List the ways in which your church communicates information. What, if anything, is still missing?
- Where can you improve on inclusion, inspiration and illustration in the way you communicate?

Collaboration

- How do you involve the whole church in processing change?
- Who might you be leaving out and why?

Consensus and compromise

- Where do you feel there is a strong consensus in the life of your church at the moment?
- Where is consensus lacking and why?
- Are there any areas where God might be calling you to compromise and submit to one another?

Character formation

- 'Not everything that is faced can be changed, but nothing can be changed until it is faced.' Are there any aspects of your church's life that you find difficult to face? When might be a good time to share and face them together?
- Change is like a relay race. Are you creating an ongoing cycle of renewing and changing the church, or are you marking out a finishing line with nothing beyond?

✣

Chapter Four

SHAPING PERCEPTIONS:
THE CHALLENGE OF CHANGE

By faith Abraham, when called to go to a place he would later receive as
his inheritance, obeyed and went, even though he did not know where
he was going. By faith he made his home in the promised land like a
stranger in a foreign country.
HEBREWS 11:8–9a

We are therefore Christ's ambassadors.
2 CORINTHIANS 5:20

It's so easy to glamorize the image of pioneers and ambassadors discovering new worlds and exotic cultures, building bridges and friendships with a view to mutual learning. Unfortunately, the image that is often conveyed by an 'out of touch' church is perhaps more like the story of the Austrian ambassador, who was attending his first official function in Vienna. There were scores of diplomats and celebrities at the event and he was understandably a little fearful and nervous. But the food was exquisite, the wine flowed freely, the orchestra played brilliantly, and eventually the atmosphere of the occasion completely overtook him, so that he was swept along with nervous excitement. He decided to invite one of the ladies to dance with him, and turned to the person sitting next to him, who was wearing a beautiful long dress, encrusted with jewels. When he asked the question, however, he was met not only with a scowl and a refusal, but with three very good reasons why it was out of the question: 'Number one, this is not a ball, it is a banquet. Number two, this is not dance music, but the Austrian National Anthem. And number three, I am not a woman, I am the Cardinal Archbishop of Vienna!'

On a more serious note, this particular image is perhaps not very far from the truth in considering how the church attempts to cope with its role of ambassador in the world today. Not only do many Christians appear to act more like refugees, fleeing from a world in which they don't feel safe and secure, but the world itself seems increasingly strange, unfathomable and ever changing. In fact, life in the 21st century has not only gone on changing at an alarming rate, but the changes themselves have been increasingly radical and bewildering. The author Isaac Asimov once said:

It is change, continuing change, inevitable change, that is the dominant factor in society today. No sensible decision can be made any longer, without taking into account not only the world as it is, but the world as it will be... This, in turn, means that our statesmen, our businessmen, our everyman must take on a science fictional way of thinking.[1]

Of course, for most of us, the words 'sensible' and 'science fiction' do not sit easily together, especially when the challenge of coping with a changing world can make us feel as if we are living on an alien planet. Apply this to a church that is in any case still living in the past, and the scale of the challenge becomes overwhelming. No wonder, then, that many churches choose to avoid even thinking about it—yet this is not an option if we are to continue as faithful disciples. Just as Abraham, 'even though he did not know where he was going', was prepared to live 'like a stranger in a foreign country', our call to be Christ's ambassadors is stronger than ever as our world continues to change. Indeed, unless we respond to the call, there will be little 'inheritance' and no 'promised land' (Hebrews 11:8–9).

We will look more closely at Abraham's story, but first let's take a moment to consider our culture and how it is shifting, along with some of the implications for the way we do church. Be warned, though, that things will have changed even further long before the book you are holding has begun to gather dust.

HOW WE NOW LIVE

The first thing to note about life today is that it has become far more flexible and at the same time more complicated, with greater levels of choice but proportionately fewer hours in which to exercise that choice. Not only have working hours increased but working partners struggle to juggle their lives around each other and their children. As the divorce rate rises, children are regularly shunted between homes, especially at weekends. Meanwhile, life has far more to offer on the leisure side, and interest in travel, hobbies, sport and shopping has escalated. Not surprisingly, the shape of one particular day, Sunday, has been transformed beyond recognition. No longer is it a boring 'do nothing' day, as in the past, when the only venues open were the pub (for a few hours) and the local church. Instead, it is one of the busiest shopping days of the week—if not the busiest—and has virtually lost all connotations of a 'day of rest'.

Where does this leave church? Attending Sunday worship is now just one of a whole range of attractive options, and the church has slowly but surely begun to recognize that it is increasingly difficult to attract newcomers on that particular day. But I wonder whether it has yet woken up to the fact that a commitment to weekly Sunday worship is also an increasingly tricky option for its core members. One of the privileges of pastoring the same church over a very long period is living through a number of changing seasons and trends in the church's life. Over more than 20 years I've watched the congregation grow into multiple services and church plants, but I've also seen a significant decrease in individual attendance. The trend has looked something like the following, and this is confirmed not only by the available studies and statistics but by many conversations with other church leaders.

Fifty years ago, committed members would attend church up to three times on Sundays. Not only would they attend morning and evening services, but many would also teach Sunday school in the afternoon or attend the men's or women's Bible classes. When I first moved to St Mark's, core members would appear twice on a Sunday, in the morning and the evening. Ten years ago, they would be solidly committed to attending once a week, every week. Since then, however, the trend has continued downwards, so that even our most committed leaders do not always appear on a Sunday.

At first, I must confess that I began to perceive this trend as a crisis of commitment, and proceeded to preach on it, as well as to beat myself up mentally for my inability to maintain sufficiently attractive, meaningful and inspirational services. I realize that this is a sad confession to make, but unfortunately many church leaders are tempted to find their security in who appears and what happens at the Sunday service. Eventually, however, I began to do what pastors are supposed to do, and sat down to listen to the stories of the people I served. I looked at their circumstances and watched their journeys, until gradually the penny dropped and I understood that the shape of Sunday worship, and of church itself, could never be the same again. Here were some of the most committed and passionate believers I knew, yet even they had understandable and excellent reasons for being unable to attend more regularly. At that point, I was very grateful that we had already sensed the importance of becoming more cell-based than Sunday-based, and that people at St Mark's could do church at different times and in more ways than one. But I also became determined that we could go much further, perhaps reinventing the way we conducted services and even the very way we gathered together, so that it not only supported but celebrated the way we all now live.

WHERE WE NOW LIVE

Another of the more significant changes of recent years is a massive increase in mobility. People today travel much further and far faster, to an ever-increasing range of destinations. When they finally arrive, more and more people make a distinction between where they buy a house and where they build a home. In other words, for many people, their local neighbourhood is simply where they choose to sleep and get some space, but what they do with others and where they actually live out the bulk of their lives happens in several other places, few of which are related in any way to their own neighbourhood. Many of us only ever meet our neighbours as they climb into their car to drive off and live their lives elsewhere. That life may consist of a career and workplace situated on the far side of town, or even the next town. They will have a range of favourite shopping venues in a range of different locations, as well as other places that they visit to pursue a hobby or to play or watch their favourite sport. And when they visit friends and family, again that will probably involve travelling far from their own neighbourhood community.

From neighbourhoods to networks

For any local church that still sees itself exclusively in neighbourhood terms, this is a seismic shift, and understandably so. A hundred years ago, the local church was at the very core of community life. Not only was there little else going on there, but their own community was all that most people ever saw or knew. They didn't have cars, trains and aeroplanes in abundance to take them to 101 different places. They had little opportunity of moving beyond their community to experience everything from shopping malls to sports stadiums, cinemas, restaurants, pubs, clubs and classes, theme parks, leisure parks and package holidays. We, unlike them, have to manage jobs, families and friendships that are no longer located on the same street, in the same town or, increasingly, the same county or country. Just as life has changed on a massive scale, so the church will have to change too, if it's going to survive.

Of course, if a church still has a reasonable Sunday congregation, it will be tempted to think that none of this affects its own particular life and future. What should haunt us, however, is that we may have a packed church in a single location and still have 10,000 neighbours living on our doorstep who will never connect with us. It's very easy to live under the illusion that we are relevant and 'seeker friendly' because of our size, when in fact we're slowly becoming more and more disconnected from the neighbourhood itself. Meanwhile, the loyalties of existing members will increasingly and inevitably be divided and tested as their own lives and networks become ever more diverse. Of course, none of this is to deny or devalue the importance of neighbourhood church, but the neighbourhood now provides only half of the narrative of people's lives, and our need to understand and engage with their daily networks is now paramount.

WHO WE NOW LIVE WITH

The answer to the question 'Who is my neighbour?' is now a fairly mind-blowing one, not only because of our expanding networks but because of the very nature of our relationships in a digital and globalized world. In a very real sense, my neighbour now is just about everybody on the planet. The combination of Internet, television and travel has brought the whole world into our homes, so that our spheres of interest and involvement have multiplied beyond recognition. Not only can we relate to people in new ways, through the likes of Skype, MySpace and Facebook, but we can sample whole new cultures with ease. The result is that we are now a multicultural society in the widest possible sense, and that is reflected at every level. We switch on our televisions and, instead of having five channels to choose from, there are now over 500. When we search for a radio station, there are many specialist ones as well as local ones, all competing with the familiar national ones. When we listen to music, we no longer make simple distinctions between rock and classical, folk and jazz; we find there are scores and scores of musical genres to choose from, each with their own particular following and subculture.

What are the implications for the way we gather and worship? A couple of generations ago, it was probably still possible to identify a common 'British culture', in which the church played an accepted role. Within that role, the church has managed to hold together a handful of traditions from which people could choose. Apart from their theological stance, they could choose between hymns and songs, canticles and choruses, organ and drums, homilies and expositions, and could go 'up the candle' or 'below the floorboards', depending on their personal taste. Presented well, we think of our worship gatherings as shop windows, giving the world a glimpse of what's on offer. Whether we intend to or not, we present people with a particular style and culture, which speaks to them about who we are and what we value, and visitors can make choices based on what they see and how it relates to them.

Several years ago, it was relatively simple to combine a range of styles and traditions and say, 'This is the church, and this is for you.' In the 1980s, I was part of a movement that brought together many churches for major festivals and outreach events, and the worship itself became a powerful and authentic tool for attracting people to faith. But what would such an event look like today? And how is it possible to speak the language and honour the codes of the many different cultures that can now be represented in a single congregation?

Both my children work professionally in the music industry. They both work with contemporary bands but at different ends of the music spectrum, one in the pop scene and one in the world of punk. In their 20s, both have a mature faith and are members of two of the largest and most vibrant churches in the UK, with band-led music and professional worship leaders. Both have served those congregations with their own musical skills. As I've followed their journey and watched them embrace their respective pop and punk cultures, however, I've also seen their growing frustration as ambassadors for Christ. For when they return to their congregations and experience the gap between secular music culture and Christian music culture, they don't feel only for the people they are wanting to reach but, increasingly, for themselves. The fact is that, for all of its melody and professionalism, even these churches are still a long way from the cultures my children now inhabit.

This is not about the clash of values (which is naturally huge), but rather about a clear and increasingly uncomfortable clash of cultures. Yet culture is a key ingredient in what attracts us and makes us feel at home. If church is to relate to all people, it needs to find many more ways to adorn its window in attracting the unchurched, as well as welcoming back those who have drifted away. The challenge of change in this area alone will surely and increasingly have an impact on every kind and size of church as we move into the future.

WHAT WE NOW LIVE FOR

In a fast-moving, complex, mobile and multicultured world, the old and simple certainties have long gone, and with them the assumption that our country is a Christian one. Not only are we now a multifaith society, but a multilayered one, where every generation is wired more differently than ever from the one before. We currently distinguish between the Builders, the Boomers, the Generation X-ers and Generation Y, and each of these sectors approach and embrace faith, commitment and church in very different ways. Until recently, we have also talked about being in a postmodern world, where the emphasis is on 'pick and mix' thinking, and choosing what is 'true for you'. For many, there is now no absolute truth or common understanding, so even the word 'postmodern' has been described as 'a makeshift word, that we use until we have decided what to name the baby'.[2] The problem is that this baby is already a tearaway toddler that no name could describe. Suffice it to say, belief of any kind is in flux, and Christian belief as a British norm is in steep decline.

Once again, the implications for churches are enormous. I have promised myself not to quote statistics (as they are bound to be out of date by the time this book is published!), but let us assume for the sake of argument that nearly half the UK population is now unchurched. This means that huge numbers of people have no residual memory of Christian worship, customs and belief, because they have either never been to church or left it a very long time ago. My wife teaches the Reception class (four- and five-year-olds) in the local primary school, and every year she gets a graphic picture of an unchurched society. As Christmas comes around, she will often find that only five out of 50 children have any concept of what the word 'Jesus' might mean at Christmas time (a perception confirmed in a survey that shows that only one in eight Britons knows the details of the Christmas story). As she builds relationships with their families, she sees again and again that it is not only the parents who have never been to church, but actually the grandparents who form the first generation of completely unchurched people. For them, their children and children's children, their response to faith and Christian liturgy could be summed up in the words of a four-year-old child who was overheard by a friend of mine saying her own version of the Lord's prayer: 'Our Father, who shouts from heaven, hello, what's your name?'

In fact, it isn't just children who innocently express their ignorance. I was once watching the television programme *Family Fortunes*, in which the public had been asked to name five things associated with Easter. In descending order, the answers were eggs, bunnies, religion, bonnets and baby chicks. 'Jesus' got the 'no' buzzer.

Frankly, we have to come to terms with the fact that many people in Britain today just do not understand church traditions, hymns, symbols and customs, because they have never been in contact with them; but they are still hungry for God (because he made them that way) and interest in spirituality is very much on the increase. So how can we rise to the challenge of change in a vastly changed world, and take a new kind of church to a newly distanced generation? The questions we are asking in this chapter are not just about the importance of changed hearts, or about changing services and buildings, but about the need to begin changing the very shape of church to suit the new context in which we find ourselves.

In the second half of this book, we will explore these issues further and suggest some dreams, visions and goals for building a new future. Meanwhile, let's be honest and realistic. These are threatening and uncomfortable issues. They challenge and disturb, and, if we're not careful, they can demoralize and confuse us. They also require large doses of wisdom, faith and grace, and a degree of raw courage. But first things first. Where exactly do we start in facing the challenge to change more radically? What do we need to put behind us, and where do we begin looking for the first step forward?

SETTING OUT OR SETTLING IN?

'They set out from Ur of the Chaldeans to go to Canaan. But when they came to Haran, they settled there' (Genesis 11:31). Abraham is an inspirational example for pioneers, yet even he had his faltering moments. In particular, he had a false start at the beginning of his journey. Called to leave everything and pioneer a new future in Canaan, he set out along a beautiful expanse of land that led down the valley of the river Euphrates. Not only was the area lush, fertile and full of pasture land for the animals he and his household took, but it was like a superhighway rather than a pioneer trail. The first part of the journey took them to Haran, a major trading town by the river. Haran was a smaller version of the city they had left behind, affluent and comfortable, and a convenient stopover before setting off into the desert. Only Abraham didn't set off again. He and his family settled down in Haran for several years before they decided to face the tougher trail towards Canaan.

LIVING AT THE CROSSROADS

Appropriately, the name 'Haran' means crossroads, and the story at this point provides us with a powerful metaphor for the challenge of change. In many ways, the Church is at a crossroads at this time. It has heard the call to renewal and, in many cases, has taken some significant steps in response. So far, it has travelled a familiar and fairly comfortable trail, reshaping its services and reordering its buildings. But the real trek still lies in front of us, and it is very much a journey of faith through the desert and into the unknown. Not only does it require a change in pace but it will almost certainly bring a change of scenery and a demanding route. In fact, it may mean that we have to keep changing our path until we can read the map correctly and reach our goal. Before that, however, we need to recognize that we are currently stuck at a crossroads, and must face up to whatever is keeping us from moving on. The following factors may be relevant.

The familiarity factor

Effectively, Haran was 'home from home', not really any different from the city Abraham had left behind. It was situated on the river and on the main trade route, and it was fertile, cultured and comfortable. It also offered the same religion, along with the same sorts of buildings, tools and customs. The next destination was very different, however, and that would involve deserts and tents and a lot of faith.

Part of the challenge of change in any context will be letting go of the familiar. To do that, we have to acknowledge that familiarity not only breeds comfort but it can also breed contempt. The danger point in any church comes when a certain degree of healthy change has happened, bringing with it a measure of ease and security. At that point, the natural instinct is to bottle the situation and label it 'do not change'—and understandably so. Unfortunately, the human instinct goes further. If unchecked, comfort will always breed complacency, which eventually spirals down into contempt. As already mentioned, there are too many full and overflowing churches that work with a familiar, proven formula for attracting people in, but use that as an excuse for never moving out and attempting something new. Too easily they equate effective welcome with the kind of cutting edge cultural relevance that is now increasingly needed. I can also think of smaller congregations that rarely see a newcomer but are complacent and comfortable as a church family, and still viable financially, and so feel no obligation to move forward.

Both types of church bring to mind two pictures that have lived on in my heart for many years. The first was given to me by a black evangelist in Soweto during the apartheid era. It was of a little black boy, sitting outside the white man's church, weeping because they wouldn't let him inside. Jesus is there and, putting his arm around the little boy, he says, 'Never mind, I know just how you feel. I've been trying to get inside that church for years!' The other picture sat in a frame in George Carey's study during his time as principal of Trinity Theological College in Bristol. It was a cartoon of a worshipping congregation, singing a hymn but oblivious of the person sitting alone on the front pew. That person was Jesus, and he was reading a newspaper.

Of course, we shouldn't need satirical pictures to point out the levels of our complacency or even contempt. What we do need, however, is a clear revelation from God as to exactly where familiarity could be leading us.

The family factor

When God had called Abraham, he'd told him to leave his father's household (Genesis 12:1), yet not only did his father Terah go with him, but we read that Terah 'took' him (11:31). Following the normal pattern of family hierarchy, Terah obviously made the running, set the course and ruled the roost. In this case, it meant delaying the call to Canaan and settling down in Haran, until he eventually died. While he was alive, Terah obviously didn't share some of his son's values, and 'worshipped other gods' (Joshua 24:2); in fact, both Ur and Haran were havens for idol worship. Now we don't know whether it was Terah's age and stage in life or his idolatry and love for Haran that conspired for a time against the Canaan vision, but we do know that Abraham didn't move on from Haran until Terah had died.

The family factor is a huge one in considering change. Our church families are not only packed with parental and patriarchal figures, who may have far less interest in the future than we have, but we also live alongside Christian brothers and sisters who may not share our values and vision. We may also come from a spiritually divided home, where our partner and family cannot understand why we want to invest so much of ourselves in the church and its future. Or it may just feel inappropriate to push an ageing and dying congregation to face and make significant changes. Either way, the family factor has to be faced, with wisdom and tact but ultimately with courage and conviction. Whatever the difficulties of Abraham's situation, the command of the Lord was still very clear—to 'leave your father's household and go'. Of course, it would be wrong to generalize and legislate here, but my instinct is that we too often allow the family factor to hold us back when God is trying to move us forward. My appeal is simply to consider it seriously and respond appropriately.

The affluence factor

The city of Ur was one of the most important and affluent cities in the ancient world. Situated on the Persian Gulf and bordered by the river Euphrates, it would have felt like the centre of the universe in commercial and cultural terms. Compared to other regions, it had the best of everything, including beautiful high-rise temples built by highly educated engineers, architects and artists. To leave this place was a sacrifice in any sense, and yet Haran was, at least, a smaller version of the same thing—attractive, affluent, safe and civilized.

While it may not always feel so to us, we should never forget that the Church in the West is affluent. It lives in buildings and often lives off assets, investments, inheritances and grants. Personally, I've found that one of the biggest vision killers in building projects appears when a congregation has a pot of money in storage and does not have to flex its faith muscles in order to build. Instead of planning with a faith mentality and asking, 'What could be?' it reverts to a budget mentality and declares 'what it can't be'. It spends according to its bank balance instead of giving according to its faith. Of course, this is not to say that savings and grants are not a blessing, but we should see them as a starting point and never a finishing line.

Even where it doesn't have money, a church can still enjoy what I'd call a pastoral affluence. Taking the definition of affluence as 'flowing freely or in great quantity', a congregation can place great value on the quality and quantity of pastoral care afforded to its own members, to the detriment of its mission. Many times I've met pastors whose main reason for their lack of vision is plainly their lack of energy. Their day-to-day ministry is so caught up with the pastoral demands of their flock that they cannot face the pressure of change at any price, not least because it will create a demand for even more pastoral attention. In the end, the affluent church should count its blessings, but not at the cost of diminishing vision. What we have and enjoy must never be allowed to blind us to what we still need, and need to live for.

DYING TO LIVE

Abraham eventually moved and became the model pioneer for generations of believers. No doubt, after several years of following his father's lead, he couldn't wait to move to Canaan when the call came again. The events of his life, however, show that he ended up learning more about sacrifice than seeing the whole of God's promise to him fulfilled.

The climax of his wandering life came with the greatest challenge of all: 'Some time later God tested Abraham. He said to him, "Abraham!" "Here I am," he replied. Then God said, "Take your son, your only son, Isaac, whom you love, and go to the region of Moriah. Sacrifice him there as a burnt offering on one of the mountains I will tell you about"' (Genesis 22:1–2).

The first thing to notice in this story is that God did not sneak up on Abraham's blind side, as it were, or trip him up when he was weak. In fact, he tested him after Abraham had spent many years journeying with God, when he was absolutely prepared for such a test, having learnt many important and helpful lessons along the way. Again, at this point, it is important to note that God meets us wherever we are on our journey and simply asks us to take another step of obedience, another step forward, even though it may seem like a very big one. Changing the shape of church may not be the immediate call on everyone's life but we are all called to be open to God's call to change and grow. Whatever form that call takes, it always involves counting the cost and being willing to make sacrifices, and there are three sacrifices in particular that pioneers of change may have to face.

The sacrifice of our common sense

Abraham had waited for years to receive his inheritance, and Isaac was the fulfilment of a God-given promise. What possible sense did it make to kill him? God's call is to follow and trust, however, and the

Bible is full of examples of his extraordinary tests and requests, all of which are about kingdom and character building.

In a similar way, Christians sometimes have to throw away the rule book of sound principles of change and apparently abandon common sense. Before we embarked on our building project at St Mark's, we had to jump over several hurdles of common sense. The commonest one is encountered when a church decides to raise funds that are way beyond its present resources. All the accounting in the world will fail to make sense, at first, of anything that genuinely calls itself a 'faith' project. Similarly, if a building is warm and functional and in good repair, it can make little sense to the average person to embark on a major reordering. Our building was beautifully cared for, so, when the bulldozers moved in and literally carved up the space, it was definitely an 'Isaac' moment. As thick black smoke belched out of the knocked-down walls, an elderly gentleman on the street waved his walking stick at me and shouted angrily, 'I'm going to report you!' At that particular point, I was feeling fairly sure that I needed not only reporting but certifying as well! It was a lonely moment, in which the sacrifice felt huge and common sense absent.

The sacrifice of our dreams

Isaac didn't just represent the fulfilment of a promise; he encapsulated all of Abraham's dreams. Sooner or later, God will ask us to offer him our most cherished possessions and aspirations, inviting us to trust him totally. The call comes in many forms, and it comes to churches as well as individuals. My own dream, for instance, was to build a large and tangible expression of renewal and life through multiple services and overflowing congregations. But when the challenge came to move more radically in mission and to experiment with radically new forms of church, we found ourselves actually closing two out of our four Sunday services to enable the change. In a way, it was a literal application of the cartoon that shows a church door locked and padlocked, with a sign saying, 'You've been coming here long enough. Now go and do it!' As we did do it, we nervously watched our Sunday attendance figures go down, and it took a couple of years before we started to see the visible fruit of such a radical move. Sometimes, we have to let go of our dream for a time, in order to fulfil the overall mission.

The sacrifice of our strengths

Isaac also represented Abraham's strengths and successes, whereas his other son, Ishmael, symbolized his weaknesses and mistakes. Having waited for years for the fulfilment of God's promise of a son, Abraham and Sarah had grown impatient, which had led to Hagar the slave girl bearing a child for Abraham. This one mistake unleashed a trail of misery (Genesis 16) as Hagar despised Sarah, Sarah blamed Abraham and mistreated Hagar, and Hagar was forced to run away. Ishmael himself, cut off from his father's love, became a 'wild donkey of a man' who, along with all his descendants, lived 'in hostility toward all his brothers' (16:12; 25:18).

When we think about it, all of us would be happy to be freed of our Ishmaels, the tragic mistakes that get reproduced and multiplied over time, and they are usually the issues that we try to surrender in prayer and for which we receive ministry. But how do you respond when God says, 'Surrender your strengths, surrender what you've poured your life into, what you think you do best, which defines you and brings you praise'? Many of the good things we now enjoy doing in ministry may well need laying down at some point, in order to embrace the future that God wants for us. Churches with a full and vibrant congregation, for instance, will often find the decision to divide and multiply an excruciatingly difficult one. One Sunday, the seats are filled and the building echoes with the voices of a praising crowd, but the next Sunday finds the congregation halved and the sound of worship a little hollow for a while. These churches will usually have to wait another year or so before they see God rewarding the offering and the congregation doubling in size. To paraphrase a famous verse (2 Corinthians 12:9), 'God's strength shows up best in weak people', in those who are prepared to sacrifice their own strengths.

BEYOND THE CROSSROADS

In one way or another, all of us stand at the crossroads of change, with God calling us onward. For some, the first part of the journey involves some basic heart surgery, and until that happens we won't be able to digest anything beyond Chapter One of this book. For others, it may mean actively planning the route to change and becoming more intentional about moving on. For many, it will mean a journey of renewal, determined to develop and enhance the church services, ministries and buildings we have already inherited. For increasing numbers of us, however, it has to mean a more radical step, from simply being pastors to becoming pioneers, from being preoccupied with maintenance to promoting and being more passionate about mission. Beyond that, we must not only learn to be shapers of change, but must embrace the possibility that we are ultimately called to shape the future, by changing the very shape of church. In the following chapters, we will explore what it might mean to become an increasingly mission-shaped church.

———— ✣ ————

MEETING THE CHALLENGE

How we now live

- What are the Sunday attendance trends in your church?
- Are there any particular factors in your context that affect people's commitments to church?

Where we now live

- What kind of networks do the people in your church belong to?
- Are there one or two types of network that are particularly strong?
- How are you engaging with them as a church?

Who we now live with

- How many different cultures are represented in your church?
- How are you catering for them?

What we now live for

- Imagine someone visiting one of your services who has never been inside a church before. Put yourselves in their shoes and think about how they would feel, what they would notice.
- Where would you need to make changes to make them feel at home?

Living at the crossroads

- Reflecting on Abraham's life at Haran, what issues might hold back your church from responding to God's call to move on?
- What practical steps can you take to respond to the challenge posed by these issues?

Dying to live

- Reflecting on the story of Abraham's call to sacrifice Isaac, where might you be called to sacrifice your common sense, your dreams or your strengths?

Chapter Five

RESHAPING MISSION

I would like to rise very high, Lord,
Above my city
Above the world
Above time.
I would like to purify my glance and borrow your eyes.
MICHEL QUOIST[1]

A few years ago, a new phrase was introduced into my vocabulary, and now it's been welded into my psyche: 'paradigm shift'. It may sound a bit pretentious but it is a unique phrase that cannot really be replaced with any other. It's defined in the dictionary as 'a fundamental change in approach or underlying assumptions', and it's a crucial phrase to grasp in our changing world. It means that we've been looking at things in a certain way, and now we're not only going to see things differently but our whole approach to the way we see is going to shift.

In *The Challenge of Cell Church*, I used the example of someone learning to snorkel for the first time. Imagine floating in the ocean, looking toward the horizon across a barren landscape of sea and sky. One small shift of the head, however, and your view of the world dramatically changes as your eyes refocus below the surface. Your location hasn't changed and you're still floating, but now you can not only see algae, coral and shoals of fish, but you have a whole new perspective on the ocean itself. Another example comes from the world of text messaging. Whenever my wife forgets to put on her glasses before sending me a text, I receive a very strange message, with words that have letters missing, or the wrong ones altogether.

Only when she's put on the right lenses and adjusted her vision do I end up reading what I'm meant to read. A third example comes from a visit I made recently to another church, where I listened to the vicar's sermon on the theme 'God has mercy'. The message was anything but merciful. I sat with a Bible on my lap, hearing the sterner parts of the passage expounded while whole sections on God's pleasure, compassion and grace were missed out. It was almost as if we were reading different Bibles; the verses and themes were clearly there but had been either skipped over as a genuine oversight or deliberately ignored. Either way, a paradigm shift was needed, somewhere between the pulpit and the pew.

Translate all that into discipleship terms, and we need to ask God to 'purify our glance' and let us 'borrow his eyes', so that we can see the world, the Church and the gospel message as he sees it. Without that paradigm shift, we'll look at our church and see only the services, clergy, home groups and social events that we've habitually been seeing and doing there for years. Similarly, we'll look at our mission and see the way we've always done it, whether that be outreach, service, witness or invitations to church. Whatever we are looking at, our vision will always be impaired in comparison to God's, so we need to ask him continually for a fresh perspective. With that in mind, I invite you to read the rest of this book with a new and invisible pair of spectacles, looking at the same old subjects with a fresh focus. It will also mean deliberately shifting your viewing position, so that the old viewpoint no longer dominates. You may even begin to discover additional things worth looking at.

We've already talked about shaping change in the Church, and the need for changing attitudes. Now we're going to explore the possibility of changing the very shape of Church, and the need for a paradigm shift in this whole area.

SHIFTING THE FOCUS

'Mission-shaped church' is one of the more helpful phrases that has been introduced in recent years, along with the phrase 'fresh expressions of church'. Both appeared in the 2004 Church of England Report,[2] and since then the phrase 'fresh expression' has been more clearly defined:

A fresh expression is a form of church for our changing culture, established primarily for the benefit of people who are not yet members of any church.

- *It will come into being through principles of listening, service, incarnational mission and making disciples.*
- *It will have the potential to become a mature expression of church shaped by the gospel and the enduring marks of the church and for its cultural context.*[3]

To be honest, the phrase 'fresh expressions' is constantly being redefined and is open to continuous reinterpretation. But the meaning of 'mission-shaped church' is not only self-evident, but simple, crisp and clear. If we're honest, many of us have been guilty of engaging in 'church-shaped mission'—of shaping our mission to fit the church to which we belong. In effect, we have said, 'This is the kind of church we are, and you're very welcome to join us. But the shape of our church and its particular tradition cannot be changed.' In truth, however, it was meant to be the other way around. The church should always have been built around and shaped by its mission, by the context and culture in which it finds itself. Standing within our culture, we should ask the question, 'What could the Church of God look like in this setting, and how can the kingdom of God be expressed in this place?' If we begin with that question, others will quickly and naturally follow, about how and when and where we should meet. No longer will we assume that one size fits all and that everything we do will have to fit inside our church building.

This approach is very different from the way so many of our churches have evolved over the last 50 years or so. In my own evangelical tradition, for instance, the emphasis in the 1960s was on crusade evangelism, on gathering people together in large numbers to hear a gifted preacher and then attracting them into the life of the church. In the 1970s, that approach evolved into local and more indigenous mission weeks and guest services, where the event itself was still hugely important. By the 1980s, a new understanding of process and friendship evangelism was developing, and in the 1990s more sophisticated initiatives, such as Alpha, emerged. All of these approaches have had and still have their place, and I have many special memories of involvement in them all. Good as they have been or still are, however, in their different ways they still work on the model of attracting people from the outside in, from their own culture into our particular church culture. Meanwhile, other parts of the Church have always put the major emphasis on being 'salt and light', living and serving in the world and taking church and kingdom values to where people are. Even so, there is still often an uncomfortable separation between worship and witness, and the gulf between effective social action and the way worship is conducted on a Sunday has, in many places, grown ever wider.

A new paradigm from an old story

In Acts 2, we're given the first vivid snapshot of a mission-shaped church. Surprisingly, it doesn't look anything like the gathering we read about at the beginning of that chapter, when Peter preaches and 3000 come to faith in a single day (v. 41). Taking that as a successful model, we might have expected to read about an ongoing crusade where, night after night, vast crowds gathered to listen to a great preacher, with a huge response to the 'altar call'. In fact, though, we read of another very different model. This model is not focused on any individual but on the *laos*, a Greek word literally translated as 'little people', and from which we get our word 'laity', meaning lay or ordinary people. Here in the second chapter of Acts, we see that it was the little people, meeting in little groups and little communities, doing little acts of service and hospitality alongside little acts of worship, who were rocking Jerusalem. It may be helpful at this point to read the passage afresh and in full, being careful not simply to pick out the elements that in some way remind us of our own church:

They devoted themselves to the apostles' teaching and to the fellowship, to the breaking of bread and to prayer. Everyone was filled with awe, and many wonders and miraculous signs were done by the apostles. All the believers were together and had everything in common. Selling their possessions and goods, they gave to anyone who had need. Every day they continued to meet together in the temple courts. They broke bread in their homes and ate together with glad and sincere hearts, praising God and enjoying the favour of all the people. And the Lord added to their number daily those who were being saved (Acts 2:42–47).

All these little things, added together, is what the New Testament calls 'fellowship', but there are two factors that made it a dynamic and powerful experience in the early Church, both for those taking part and for the people around them. First of all, it was happening out in the community, not in the sacred space of the temple. Secondly, they were doing all these little things in a very big way. They weren't just gathering on the sabbath, but seeing each other every day. They didn't just sing and pray together, but they ate, shared and gave of themselves generously. The passage also makes some very challenging points about this little thing called 'fellowship'. It says that 'all the believers' did it, not just those who felt like it or who didn't have demanding families or busy jobs. It says that they had 'everything in common', not just a vicar and a congregation. It also says that they 'devoted themselves' to it; they didn't simply discuss and consider it, and occasionally decide in its favour.

The Church today has often diluted the word 'fellowship' until it ends up meaning something completely different. We talk about the men's or women's fellowship, by which we mean a meeting or gathering that men or women are welcome to join if they feel so inclined. We talk about 'having fellowship' after a service or over a coffee, and it's a very pleasant word and sounds a nice, friendly thing to do with other believers. As we might guess, however, the word 'fellowship' in the New Testament is a far stronger word, with a wider, more powerful meaning. The Greek word used is *koinonia,* meaning 'everything we share in common', and, as lived out by the early Church, it was intoxicatingly attractive. In fact, the phrase that stands out strikingly in the passage above is the one that describes them 'enjoying the favour of all the people' (v. 47). The implication is that when the Church is the kind of community it is supposed to be, it finds favour in the wider community and begins to find its true shape and destiny.

Unfortunately, we have sometimes chosen to imply the opposite. In fact, I come from a tradition that seemed at times to hint that if I enjoyed any kind of favour with the world, I was probably sinning. The inference was that Christians were meant to stand out as different in a hostile 'worldly' environment, so they should not be surprised if they never experienced people's favour, and they probably wouldn't feel like praising God, either! Acts 2 begins by emphasizing the natural magnetism of an authentic Christian community, and only in the wake of that do the inevitable battles come. The primary impact, before the religious authorities react in opposition, is one of favour, which stems from the community of believers 'sharing what they have in common' with the ordinary people.

At the same time, we should note that *koinonia* did not have just religious connotations; it was used widely to describe the bonds of relationship within any community. The Church, however, put a whole new perspective on the word, and it was the Church's particular brand of *koinonia* that became the key to unleashing the love of God into a needy world.

SHARING WHAT WE HAVE IN COMMON

Apart from sharing a need for God's love and grace, Christians have many things in common with the people they encounter in daily life. Christians also have natural and God-given passions and interests that take up much of their lives and their time apart from the Church. For some, it's a hobby like painting, photography or walking, or belonging to a particular community hub, like the local pub or social club. For others, their passion is in playing or watching sport at the regional cathedral of soccer, rugby or cricket. Meanwhile, for many people, their main passion is their work, and they spend most of their waking hours immersed in it, revelling in the buzz, security and sense of belonging it brings. For as many more, their energy simply comes from home and neighbourhood and their role as parent, neighbour or community friend. And then, of course, there's always a core group in the church who devote the majority of their life and energy to its ministries.

The fact is that all of us are pulled in a number of different directions in life. Sadly, however, we have often criticized each other for a lack of commitment and church–life balance, when we should have been celebrating our diversity of interests. Depending on our church background, we're tempted to berate people either for not spending enough time in church or for not having enough unchurched friends and outside interests. Of course, every Christian is called to commitment and community, both in and outside the church, and it is always a challenge to find the right balance. The key point, however, is that the God-given pull on our lives will draw us primarily to the areas where we're most likely to thrive. Once we find those areas, we begin to share with others what we have in common, easily and naturally, including our need for God.

Here, then, is the paradigm shift. What if the call on our lives is not just to be witnesses in the places where we live and thrive? What if our God-given pull is about becoming more than that? What if it is about actually building church and *koinonia* in new places, taking what we have in common as believers, harnessing what we have in common with non-believers, and creating a fresh expression of church, one that is truly mission-shaped and connected to the culture we're in? Let's look at some stories of doing church in new ways; as you read, do remember that we're talking about additions to, not a dismantling of, the church we have known, loved and inherited.

Famlegh First: a church in the world of education

When our family first arrived in Haydock, we planted a congregation in the local primary school, Legh Vale. We followed good practice in church planting as we understood it at the time. This meant that we gathered a team together, took the best of what we did in the church on a Sunday morning and transferred it into the school. The model was fine and the congregation grew, but the church didn't really have much impact on the school community itself. Essentially, we had moved our church culture into the school building, whenever it was empty, and school continued separately from Monday to Friday. Eventually, after the church was reordered, we left the school and regrouped for a time in the new church building, developing a multi-congregation model instead.

Fifteen years later, we planted again into the same school; this time, though, it looked dramatically different. The aim was to connect as a church with the school community itself, but not by the traditional route of using assembly and teaching slots. By now, there was a small group of Christian teachers, classroom assistants, parents and grandparents who were all part of the life of the school, and the school itself was actively looking for community partnerships. Interestingly, the group was led by my wife, Joy, who over the years had deliberately followed her passion for children and invested the greater part of her life and ministry there. In fact, she'd become far better acquainted with the local families than her husband, the vicar, ever had, and over the years had won the affection and respect of the people she'd served. Not surprisingly, then, when she announced a new venture for the school community, it had an immediate and direct impact. They knew she was the vicar's wife and, more importantly, a Christian herself, so there was a natural assumption that something called 'Famlegh First', which met on a Sunday morning, would have God in it. What was important for them, however, was the relationship and trust that already existed, along with the 'what we have in common' element.

'What we have in common' is evident in the very shape of Famlegh First. When people arrive, they enter a familiar school culture that goes beyond the way the chairs are arranged. There is a theme each week, and various activity stations are placed around the school hall. Parents are encouraged to sit with their children and draw, paint, cut and create things based around the theme. The difference is that each station not only has a purpose and a message, but many of them are effectively prayer stations, where prayers are drawn and painted in creative ways. The activities continue for 40 minutes or so, and then they all gather together for Circle Time, when a little worship is introduced and the week's theme explained. Again, Circle Time is very much a normal part of school culture, so the safe and familiar environment releases these unchurched families to explore faith for the very first time and in a very natural way.

Let me say here that this was all rather humbling for somebody who prided himself on being a child-friendly vicar! Having spent years trying to develop state-of-the-art all-age Sunday services, it's amazing for me to see the very families who rejected every invitation to church now engaging with God and growing in faith. Increasingly, these families are also connecting in other ways, gathering together in smaller groups to share a meal, explore the faith and support each other as families. *Koinonia* takes on a whole new meaning in this context, where fellowship between God, believers and the unchurched produces community as God intended.

New Creations: a church in the world of crafts

Janet had been a Reader and church leader for many years, and also ran a cell group. Much of her life was devoted to church ministry, but she also had a passion for making cards. Once she began to share that passion, she gathered together a nucleus of 40 or so local people who all wanted to learn the craft and find community too. As a good cell leader, she also wanted to make a connection between her craft friends and Christian friends, so she extended many invitations to her cell group, all of which were politely declined.

One day, we began to apply the 'what we have in common' principle and dream of what church might look like in the setting of her card group, and where it might begin. The natural starting point came with the seasons. As Christmas approached, they started to make Advent cards, and Janet gave a little introduction on the meaning of Advent. She did it briefly and tentatively, asking whether people minded as she moved around the tables after her little talk. To her surprise, they were not only enthusiastic but the explanation opened up the most natural conversations about what was happening in their lives, and where God and faith fitted in. Before long, they asked her to talk more about spiritual things, and again we looked at the context to see how this might develop.

We noticed that many of the group members met for lunch before the craft session, so Janet invited them to gather over lunch to go on exploring faith. Two small groups were soon formed. Again, the groups didn't follow a church format; they simply picked up on the issues that they currently had in common. At the first meeting, they talked about their families and how little they saw of their grandchildren. Because of this, one woman in particular was struggling with a strained relationship with her daughter. Gently and at the appropriate time, Janet dropped a single verse from Isaiah into the middle of the conversation. In the Good News Bible, it reads, 'Can a woman forget her own baby and not love the child she bore? Even if a mother should forget her child, I will never forget you… I have written your name on the palms of my hands' (Isaiah 49:15–16). Later in the meeting, the woman said, 'I suppose I've been treating God the way I feel my daughter has been treating me.' She now plays a full part in the whole life of our church. She also has a vibrant faith.

New Creations, as Janet's card-making project is called, has all the potential to become a church in its own right. Already, the pastoral and worship life of the groups has developed and easy connections have formed with traditional church as well. Out of those who have come to faith, several have been confirmed and now attend Sunday services, one or two others have connected with Famlegh First instead, and the remaining few attend New Creations and nothing else, happily calling it their church. The important thing has been to put in the building blocks, one by one, never assuming what church has to look like and always embracing what the people involved have in common.

Riverforce: a church in the world of work

Peter and his Christian friends had a prodigious ability to invite their colleagues in the police force to their cell group. As it grew and multiplied, we used to call it the police cell! Even for him, however, it became increasingly difficult to invite people to travel 20 miles from his network in the city to his neighbourhood church.

One day, I suggested the possibility of planting a church in the network itself. Potentially, this consisted of a community of around 500 people working at police headquarters, and another 5000 around the region. Peter introduced me to the Assistant Chief Constable, responsible for personnel and welfare in the force. He had been thinking about pastoral care, obviously aware of the chaplaincies and Christian Unions that exist in many workplaces. Our suggestion was to take it further, however, and gradually introduce the building blocks of church. He was very open to the idea, saying that it was the first time he had ever gone to a meeting with his own agenda and come away with someone else's.

I was amazed at how quickly and smoothly the vision was embraced. Within a couple of weeks, we met with five other senior officers, and I was struck by the spiritual hunger in the room. Most of them had had some kind of connection with the church or with some other form of spirituality, but their demanding shift-based jobs had drawn most of them away from traditional patterns of church attendance. Here was a group of people with very real pastoral needs, ranging from illness and bereavement to relationship breakdowns and stress of all kinds. In fact, the desire to engage with what we were offering was so strong that they immediately agreed to form the first cell group. This was no easy task, as they were all working exceptionally long hours, but they still agreed to meet on a regular basis. From there, the vision quickly took hold, until several cell groups were meeting and other forces across the country were enquiring about the model. What has struck me about this particular experience is the simple power of networks: when something is offered that suits the culture and fits the context, the speed of ownership is phenomenal.

Riverbank: A church in the world of community groups

Moss Bank is a village community with a hall at its centre. Various creative groups meet there regularly to pursue their hobbies and interests. Among them are two Christian couples, who between them lead a craft group, a painting group, a photography group, a walking group and a group supporting relief aid around the world. They are not only very artistic but also well connected and passionately concerned about the quality of community life.

To harness such enthusiasm and creativity is a dream project for any church planter. Once again, the vision for doing church in new ways ignited immediately because the passion and the gifts fitted the context so easily. We agreed that a 'café church' model would be best suited to the creative feel of the groups, and very soon the hall was filled with the sounds of ambient music, the aroma of fresh coffee and a small crowd of people relaxing on wicker chairs with their Sunday newspapers. Into this relaxed setting was injected a five- or ten-minute thought for the day—what I like to call a 'snapshot of faith' to whet people's spiritual appetite. Before long, the monthly café went fortnightly, with an additional gathering called Café Plus, where the building blocks of worship, prayer and teaching were introduced. Soon after that, small groups began to form for those who were now embracing a newfound faith.

Although this project was initiated by a larger, well-resourced church, the small local parish church got involved and gave it their blessing. A couple from the church joined the leadership team and became fully involved, which effectively enabled a very traditional church to start engaging in a fairly radical venture. It didn't sap their own resources but it did begin to offer a new future for a tiring and struggling congregation.

Tango: a church in the world of community support

Tango ('Together As Neighbours Giving Out') was spawned by a small group of people led by Avril, who was moved and motivated by the deprivation that dominates whole sections of our community. Under her leadership, they built up a thriving ministry, connecting with scores of families, opening a common meeting place and providing clothing, food and furniture on a huge scale. Again, the emphasis was on 'what we have in common' (in this case, a common concern for the disadvantaged), and again the building blocks of church were put in place, with cell groups, pastoral care and a worship gathering in the local pub.

As it developed, the feeling had emerged that our own church building would quite frankly feel too 'posh' for many of the Tango clientele, so an alternative venue was set up. Fascinatingly, both church and Tango offer lunches each day, situated on opposite sides of the same road, both consistently busy, yet offering startlingly different menus, prices and approach. Each of them is working with 'what we have in common' but with two very different cultures that exist on opposite sides of the same parish fence. They are also operating out of the vision and gifts of one person, who happens to have a passion for hospitality, a lifelong connection with church and community, and an even bigger heart for the poor.

WHAT'S ON OUR HEART?

You may have noticed the repeated use of similar words in this chapter, words like 'energy', 'buzz', 'thrive', 'devote', 'enthusiasm' and especially 'passion'. Passion is the secret ingredient that infuses power into every mission project, and it comes directly from God. But how does it appear and what does it look like? No doubt most of us will have heard sermons on it and been challenged to get more of it, but it may be that we've had the wrong perspective on it. Perhaps we have talked about the need to be more passionate in our witness, welcome and proclamation of the gospel, while failing to affirm the natural and spontaneous passions that already make us who we are.

Each of us has a God-given 'shape', helpfully explained by Rick Warren as a fivefold SHAPE consisting of our Spiritual gifts, our Heart and passion, our natural Abilities, our Personality, and the sum of our Experiences. What is striking in the above stories is that each and every leader had simply been released to make the most of their own personal 'shape'. Instead of being challenged to be more passionate about their witness, they were simply given the chance to express their particular passions, but in a missionary way and in a mission context. Perhaps this is a little closer to the heart of God.

What's on God's heart?

Any theology of mission or of God, for that matter, must begin with the fact that he is essentially a missionary God, a searching and sending God who tirelessly and passionately reaches out in love. Throughout the Bible story, we see movement outward, with God reaching further and deeper into the world in all its brokenness. Even after the Fall, when Adam and Eve were expelled from Eden, God continued following, chasing, seeking and moving after his people, raising up patriarchs, prophets and leaders to gather them, teach them and guide them towards a promised land. In fact, it was only as they were dragged into exile that they began to understand the full extent to which Yahweh was still following them. Even in Babylon, God was present and on the move, anticipating a new future for his people as he brought a message of hope and deliverance through the prophets Daniel and Ezekiel.

When the Church is finally born, we see the searching and sending God still at work, with 'waves of the Spirit' rippling toward the far reaches of the earth. In fact, when we look at the very nature of the Trinity we see the same movement, as the Father sends the Son, who then sends the Spirit, who together send the Church.

What's at the heart of our mission?

The more we look at how God has been at work in history, the more ridiculous it seems that we should ever have tied him down to a church building and a fixed liturgy, not to mention a programme of 'mission events' aiming to attract people in. Perhaps it's more tragic, however, that we have also failed to recognize the hand of a missionary God at work in our ordinary lives. We may talk about receiving his Spirit, sharing his heart and inviting him into our lives, and then we understandably look for the fruit and the gifts that he promises his children (John 14—15). But when we look for the signs of his working in our lives, what do we expect to see? Should we not expect it to be making us more authentically mission-shaped, connecting with the passions we already have for our work and our play, our homemaking and hobbies? Or are we so blinkered by our traditional images of what professional evangelists, vicars and worship leaders do that we cannot see what a mission-shaped Christian actually looks like?

Whether or not we recognize it, God has given us a mission-shaped heart, because that is what his own heart is like, but he gifts us in line with our personality. The people in the stories in this chapter come from very different backgrounds and perspectives, yet their experiences all speak of a mission-shaped God. The New Testament offers us a wonderful image of the Church's unity and diversity, using the image of the body of Christ and applying it specifically to our different gifts. I dare to wonder how Romans 12 might read if it were applied to our personal passions and interests:

We have different passions, according to the grace given us. If our passion is our hobby, let us use it in mission-shaped ways in proportion to our faith. If it's our work, let us work diligently and missionally; if it's in church, let us look and serve outwardly… Wherever your passion is, never be lacking in zeal, but keep your spiritual fervour, serving the Lord! (Based on vv. 6–11)

The fact that we are all different will mean that each of us is called to be a missionary in our own particular way. Some of us will be called to build the church in familiar and inherited ways, which nevertheless reach those currently outside the church. Some will begin to see their place of work with more of a mission-shaped eye, while others will get a fresh perspective on the potential in their interests and hobbies. Meanwhile, we all need to recognize the mission-shaped heart that is beating somewhere within each one of us. As we do, we may begin to ask the kind of questions that a young and inquisitive camel once asked of his father:

'Dad, why have we got such big flat feet?'

'Well, son, we need them in the desert because they help us to keep on our feet where the sand is so soft.'

'And why have we got big eyelashes?'

'Well, son, whenever there's a heavy wind in the desert and the sand gets thrown around in the air, we need big eyelashes to stop the sand getting into our eyes.'

'So why have we got a hump back?'

'We have a hump back because out in the desert we have no water, so our hump is designed to store lots of water and help us to survive there.'

'Dad, now I know why we have big feet, long eyelashes and a huge hump. But why are we in London Zoo?'

Like those camels, you and I have been given the humps, feet and eyelashes that make us better suited to the desert than the zoo. Quite simply, we need to be the people we were created to be, sharing our natural interests and passions, and using our humps, feet and eyelashes to connect in very natural ways with ordinary people. Only then will we discover what it really means to be mission-shaped, and only there will we fully unleash the extraordinary power of *koinonia*.

---- ✢ ----

MEETING THE CHALLENGE

- Would you describe your church as 'mission-shaped' or 'church-shaped' in its mission?
- If your church were to consider starting a 'fresh expression' of church in a different context, where would the natural opportunities (as opposed to the needs) be?
- Which of the 'fresh expressions' of church described in this chapter interest you and why? How does it spark ideas for your own situation?

- What are your natural passions and interests outside of the church context? Where are you most naturally a witness and ambassador? How could you be more open to becoming mission-shaped in that context? Could you imagine a 'fresh expression' of church there? What would it look like?

❖

Chapter Six

REDESIGNING CHURCH

[Jesus] told them this parable: 'No one tears a patch from a new gar-ment and sews it on an old one. Whoever does will have torn the new garment, and the patch from the new will not match the old. And no one pours new wine into old wineskins. If anyone does, the new wine will burst the skins, the wine will run out and the wineskins will be ruined. No, new wine must be poured into new wineskins. And none of you, after drinking old wine, wants the new, for you say, "The old is better."'
LUKE 5:36–39

Changing garments

This little passage reminds me of my father, for two reasons. It reminds me, first of all, of the Armani jeans he bought me. Being the best jeans I ever owned, I used to keep patching them as they grew more and more worn, until the material was so badly frayed and the patches so numerous that the jeans could best be described as manky rather than Armani. The various versions of Jesus' parable point out that patching up the old with the new is never good for either garment. For a start, it's nonsense to take a newly fashioned and functional garment and start cutting pieces out of it, yet that is what we often do when we encounter a new development in the wider church. We may go along to a praise celebration, for instance, and come away with a vision for free-flowing contemporary worship. Instead of taking the model off the peg and developing it, however, we patch a couple of badly linked, organ-led songs on to a traditional and already crowded liturgy and attempt to renew the worship with it. Meanwhile, we are clearly ruining the ethos and traditions upon which that service was originally built. Either way, neither the old nor the new has benefited, and both have somehow been mutilated. That is not to say that the two cannot and should not be blended together, but thoughtless patching is never the answer. Often, it is better for both to be kept distinct and separate, free to develop their own particular style.

Changing wines

Another image in this parable is of old wine, and again my father comes to mind. His idea of creating a vintage wine was to take an ordinary bottle and allow it to age, assuming that the longer he left it, the more it would mature. One Christmas, he opened a bottle of wine with a 'Dad' vintage of 20 years or so, and the smell was rancid and the taste revolting. But of course, any wine, however vintage, will eventually become undrinkable with the passage of time. Similarly, any church that rests on its laurels and considers its traditions to be of an untouchable vintage will discover one day that its 'taste and see' credentials have decayed and died. There is a huge difference between old and vintage, and the challenge is to taste and enjoy vintage at its peak, but also to know when it has passed its sell-by date and should be discarded.

Alongside the old comes the image of new wine, still fermenting and giving off carbon dioxide, and needing the elasticity of a new wineskin to allow it to develop its full promise. The fact is that any new idea or vision needs a measure of flexibility, space and time in order to mature and develop. The picture is of something that is still expanding, not yet mature but full of taste and promise. Fresh expressions of church are just like new wine: they are fresh and unfinished, as well as being an expression of church as opposed to the final and definitive version. Older wine, of course, is generally more popular and perceived to be more palatable, but the point here is that, for good reason, God chooses to pour out new wine with the potential to become a new vintage, and we need to make room for it.

Changing wineskins

The final image in Jesus' parable is of the wineskins, and he speaks of the fact that new wine and old wineskins don't generally go together. Old wineskins have dried up, hardened and stiffened with age, until they're no longer flexible enough to contain a volatile young wine. Applying the metaphor, we can imagine a church that stops listening to and feeding on God's word and begins to dry up. It grows harder and drier until, finally, it stiffens so much that it cannot move at all. Things that can't bend are more prone to breaking and ultimately being abandoned.

It's interesting to note, though, that old wineskins can actually be softened again by being soaked in oil, and Jesus was by no means writing off the old altogether. In fact, Matthew 9:17 makes the pertinent point that when you keep new wine and old wineskins separate, 'both are preserved'. In other words, it's not about 'in with the new and out with the old'. God's purpose is to nurture the new and the vintage together, harnessing the benefits of both so that both are preserved.

Changing metaphors

If we put all this together, wine making in God's kingdom can begin to look a little tricky, if not overwhelming. How do we handle the new, the old and the vintage? How do we develop new wineskins and what do we do with the old ones? How do we celebrate the energy of new wine while still enjoying the depth and maturity of the vintage kind? How do we ensure that all our wines are developing to their best potential, and are we confident that they all contain something of the gospel we love?

To answer these questions, we must change the metaphor from wine making to building, and think about the principles we will need in order to start reordering and redesigning church. Whatever we design, we want the finished product to be something that can build on the past, adapt and expand in the present and point towards the future. I want to focus on five principles of design in particular, under the headings of style, size, shape, structure and space. Each of these can be applied to any church but are particularly helpful in considering new forms of church.

FIRST PRINCIPLE: DOING IT WITH STYLE

What is the most appropriate style for a 21st-century church? Church leader Gerald Coates once said, 'God will not be tied down to seventeenth-century language, eighteenth-century songs, nineteenth-century morality, or twentieth-century jargon.'[1] We might go on to add '21st-century technology'—but the key word here for a mission-shaped church is 'variety'. If our call is to connect with every culture and engage in any context, then our challenge is to embrace a whole variety of styles in the way we do church, and not to be tied down by any one.

One of the occupational hazards of being a pioneer and an advocate of change is that people hear you expounding the more radical and unfamiliar aspects of a vision and quickly assume that the baby is being thrown out with the bath water. The baby, in this case, is the church that we have inherited and loved, and that still works for thousands of people. Let's be very clear, however, that the challenge of change is not about discarding and replacing but about adding to and renewing what is already there. It is a 'both/and' vision that embraces both inherited and emerging church, contemporary and traditional, as well as neighbourhoods and networks. What it doesn't embrace is the notion that simply doing things as they have always been done is still acceptable. However effective our worship traditions have been, if nearly half the current population has never been able to engage with them, then at least half of how we do church ought to change. We cannot afford to go on putting mission-shaped patches on church-shaped traditions. What we can do is to offer a wider variety of clothes to suit an ever-increasing range of needs.

Creating a new wardrobe

Some time ago, St Mark's decided to change its wardrobe. Although it had already refocused its life around its small groups, and although those groups were seriously trying to reach out to others, some of our group members were finding that they had little in common with each other apart from their faith. When it came to welcoming and witnessing, they struggled to work out what they had in common that they could share with their unchurched friends. For example, if the leader suggested having a quiz night at the local pub, half would complain that they didn't like quizzes and the other half would complain that they didn't like pubs. And when someone suggested going out for a Chinese meal, there were as many who preferred Indian, Italian or plain old fish and chips. They all shared the same values and vision for the church, but their lifestyles beyond the church were poles apart in terms of style and culture.

Increasingly, as we began to grapple with the challenge of becoming more mission-shaped, we began to pay more attention to each other's 'shape' and styles, and realized that we had to start gathering together in new ways in order to be better oriented for mission. So far, we had come to value the need for outward-looking groups, but now we began to recognize the potential for different styles of groups, which were focused from the outside in. Slowly but surely, we began to develop a new kind of cell group alongside what we already had. The current groups were called core cells, because they began from the core life and culture of the congregation and moved outwards. We now began to add cluster cells, groups that would begin with people clustering together outside the church setting, around a common missional focus. Each of the mission-shaped projects described in the last chapter began with a cluster cell approach, and together they offered not only a fresh approach to mission but also a refreshing variety in terms of style and taste.

'Taste and see' culture

An important word that we need to take on board here is 'consumerism'. Like it or not, we now live in a consumer world that dictates the way in which people respond to everything, including the Church. Broadly speaking, previous generations saw themselves primarily as producers, whose core value was the importance of progress. That has now given way to a world of consumers, who are far less interested in progress than in choice. Consumerism has been described as the religion of the 21st century, where everything we do and believe is seen primarily as a consumer choice. However we might be tempted to rail against the idea, the fact is that every churchgoing believer is also an avid consumer. We choose where we want to worship and at what time. We choose between different streams, traditions and denominations, and we even choose our clergy and the Sundays on which we'll attend. When we do attend, we choose where to sit, what to give and when to join in. Churches already offer a wealth of choice, but the choices are geared to the faithful and are rarely aimed in the direction of those with no faith.

What I am advocating, then, is a fresh consideration of the importance of choice and variety in reaching the unchurched, not in terms of the truth we proclaim but in terms of the way in which we proclaim it. By all means, let's continue with the contemporary and traditional styles that already work for us, but let's begin to work on new styles that are less church-shaped and more mission-shaped.

And as we do that, let's be prepared to create new wardrobes and not simply patch up the old clothes.

SECOND PRINCIPLE: DEALING WITH SIZE

Those who are already struggling with the attempt to juggle even one or two styles of worship may think it impossible and unreasonable even to consider a variety of ways of doing church. Perhaps it's OK to focus on variety and choice in a larger church, where available resources are on a par with, say, a department store, but surely not when you're struggling to run what feels like a corner shop? The challenge of change on this scale is only for the bigger players, isn't it?

Small is beautiful

Let's go back to a familiar parable.

'What shall we say the kingdom of God is like, or what parable shall we use to describe it? It is like a mustard seed, which is the smallest seed you plant in the ground. Yet when planted, it grows and becomes the largest of all garden plants, with such big branches that the birds of the air can perch in its shade' (Mark 4:30–32).

The encouraging principle here is that God not only values 'small' but has designed his kingdom in such a way that sowing and multiplying small things produces the greatest possible harvest. In fact, nowhere in the Bible do we find a mandate for planting ready-made churches. Instead, we see an emphasis on disciples making disciples, and missional communities growing out of that principle. Just as a mother could never give birth to a fully grown adult, the Church is designed to reproduce itself from the smallest seed, planted and nurtured in a secure environment, then released into the world. In his book

Organic Church,[2] Neil Cole shows how scripture repeatedly affirms the idea that harnessing just two or three people in fellowship and ministry is a potentially powerful combination. Mission (Luke 10:1), community (Ecclesiastes 4:9–12), accountability (1 Timothy 5:19), confidentiality (Matthew 18:15–17), flexibility—that is, the ease with which meetings can be arranged (Matthew 18:20), communication (1 Corinthians 14:26–33), direction (2 Corinthians 13:1) and leadership (1 Corinthians 14:29) are all stronger when the church begins to value and operate out of its minimum size. It is almost as if the Godhead itself both illustrates and promotes the principle, as it exists together in a community of three and encourages the body of Christ to do the same.

All of the stories we looked at in the last chapter were born out of an alliance and a community of two or three people. The success of those projects did not primarily depend upon their numbers, gifts and training, or even the available resources. The key ingredients were a combination of their connectedness to a particular community, their natural passions within it, and the mutual support and commitment of just two or three people. How those people are connected to and supported by the wider church is an important question that we'll return to, but suffice it to say that the mustard seed principle is a crucial component in building churches, and that can only be good news for every church, whatever the size.

Size matters

Christian Schwarz's 'Natural Church Development' project was an important piece of research on what makes churches grow.[3] In it, he discovered that smaller churches were generally more healthy than large ones, and that large size was the third most negative factor in relation to health and growth, alongside traditionalism. There is no doubt that 'multiplying more of' is preferable to 'bigger and better', but that is not to decry the importance of larger gatherings.

Bill Beckham, in his book *The Second Reformation*,[4] imagines the Church as a two-winged bird that needs the balance of both wings to be able to fly. Take away one wing and the bird will effectively be earthbound, only ever flying in circles. The Church, he argues, has two wings that keep it in balance, one of which is made up of many smaller gatherings, and one where it comes together in a single larger gathering. Together, these wings represent both the transcendent and the immanent nature of God's character, his greatness and his nearness.

These two aspects of church are often called cell and celebration, and together they offer a firm and solid foundation on which to build church. The smaller gathering allows for greater intimacy, variety, flexibility and mobility, while the larger gathering provides a focus for strength and unity, as well as a context for the sharing of vision and resources. Whatever their shape, more and more churches are recognizing and working on this fundamental balance between smaller groups and larger gatherings.

THIRD PRINCIPLE: DRAWING THE SHAPE

You will have already noticed that, as we begin to take on board any one of these principles, a dozen or so questions will follow, each demanding a little more detail and qualification. In particular, any discussion on the shape of church will very quickly move to the question, 'What is church?' At what stage can we claim that the community we're building is fully church, and how do we go about defining it? Of course, volumes have been written on the question, 'What is church?' but thankfully the answer, in essence, is quite simple and can be defined in three words: worship, community and mission. People have different ways of describing it, but essentially they are saying the same thing. Laurence Singlehurst talks about the church's purpose being to love God, love one another and love the lost. Michael Frost draws on the portrait we're given in Acts 2 and describes it as communion, community and commission. Steve Croft sees the three essential elements in being church as people, the risen Christ and mission to God's world. Neil Cole takes the letters DNA and describes church as responding to Divine truth, Nurturing relationships and Apostolic mission. The one I love best, however, is the simplest of all, and is promoted by Mike Breen in his *Lifeshapes* programme.[5] For him, the shape of church is triangular, and is expressed in three simple words: up, in and out.

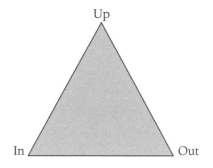

In and out of shape

The 'up, in, out' model is particularly helpful in measuring the authenticity of new and unfamiliar forms of church, but it can be applied to any church model. It can also be applied to any group or ministry within the church and used as a very effective health check on the balance of life to be found there. The smallest glance at each of these three areas will offer a fairly sharp appraisal of the effectiveness of a particular church or group. From experience, I know that, at any given time, my own church will probably be a little weaker in one area than the other two. I can also think of churches in which their strength in two of the areas is negated by their weakness in the third. Some churches place great value on the quality and quantity of worship, teaching and evangelism, but pay little attention to the quality of their relationships and their attitudes to one another. Little wonder, then, that their back door is bigger than their front door, as people gradually become disillusioned with the atmosphere within. Or we may know of churches that value community and mission but ignore the potential of worship to heal, transform and empower. Consequently, the overall life of the church is weak and unhealthy, and faith and vision are small.

Getting into shape

As the vision for new ways of doing church has gathered momentum, I've heard endless discussions on whether a 'fresh expression' is church or not, and I've even heard the question used as an argument against attempting change. It is essential to remember that planting and building any church is a process. The important thing is to be able to measure that process and focus on achievable goals. Using 'up, in, out' is a helpful and effective way of doing that. A new project may simply begin as a fresh expression of community, and may look as though it is a long way from being authentically 'church'. Add the other two components, however, and over a period of time the fully grown church will emerge and take its place on the kingdom map.

On the other hand, a fresh expression of worship, community or mission may never move beyond offering just one of the three components, and its value then must be measured in terms of its connection to the wider church. In fact, George Lings (director of the Sheffield Centre, the Church Army's research unit) has added a fourth component to the 'up, in, out' model, with the word 'of'.[6] When he speaks about this, he rightly points out that any church community is always and only authentic in so far as it is connected and grafted into the wider universal Church. Not surprisingly, then, at this point we must turn to the whole question of structures.

FOURTH PRINCIPLE: DESIGNING STRUCTURES

So far, as we've looked at the style, size and shape of church, we have emphasized the importance of variety, multiplicity and simplicity. The problem is that when we start trying to apply all of this alongside what we already have, it begins to look anything but simple. If we put together the principles presented here, we are talking of designing something that values many styles and is of different sizes, all engaging in different ways and at different levels with various forms of worship, community and mission. In addition, any fresh expression of church, by definition, will inevitably challenge and stretch our traditional structures, especially if it grows out of a network or culture that is not part of the church. By its very nature, it will cross at least three types of traditional church boundaries. First, it will cross geographical boundaries and begin to challenge our parish structures. It will also cross denominational boundaries, simply because the mission is focused on the context and not on the local church. Planting a church in the workplace, for instance, may well gather a core team of two or three people from different denominations, all of whom are now connected and called to the same mission context. And finally, it may even cross traditional leadership boundaries. For instance, when I enter the police community as a pioneer minister, I am then accountable to the Chief Constable as well as the bishop, along with any other denominational leaders who happen to be involved. Suddenly, we are dealing with a matrix of responsibility, accountability, communication and community. Putting all these issues together, the challenge of change can look enormous. Unless we address the design of our structures, any vision is likely to be strangled by them, however committed and united the church itself might be.

In the next chapter, I want to address this further in the context of leadership. Remaining for the moment on the theme of structures, there is one principle that overrides all others—the importance of flexibility. Just as new wine requires soft and flexible wineskins, new shapes of church require soft and flexible structures that provide plenty of 'give' for the moulding, movement and momentum of new life. To make that happen, three key issues should be borne in mind: pruning, purpose and power.

Pruning

As far as I am concerned, learning the principle of pruning has been one of the most liberating lessons in a long and often complicated ministry. Too often, we embrace a new idea and begin our fresh ventures in addition to all that is already happening, and then wonder why we burn out. As I write, I've just been watching television coverage of a huge burning building. The place had obviously had several quirky extensions built on to it over several generations. Not only had this made the building look very ugly, but it had also made it impossible for the emergency services to handle the fire. Wherever they tried to enter, they were met with a rabbit warren of narrow corridors and impossible bends, all tagged on with no design and little common sense. Looking at that burning building, I'm so glad that before we reordered our church building, we reviewed its whole design and then pruned the space of its pews and partitions, along with the parts that were rotten and beyond repair. The result was an open, well-proportioned and welcoming space that was attractive, adaptable and functional for a much wider range of events, as well as for further building development in future.

Since then, I have learnt to look at our church structures in the same way. Before we think of adding on services, ministries, programmes or events, we look at what we can afford to lose and dismantle in order to build again. C.S. Lewis once used a similar image of demolition and rebuilding to describe how God rebuilds the house of our lives. He reflected that we would probably be content with 'a decent little cottage' but God is wanting to build 'a royal palace' for his own purpose, so he cheerfully puts us through the pain of knocking down a few walls and reshaping the house until it is fit for his purpose.[7] We need a similar vision for renewal and growth and ongoing transformation; we also need to accommodate a creative builder-king who will constantly review, dismantle and redesign.

Purpose

Structures exist only to serve a purpose, and the key word here is 'serve'. Good structures support, strengthen, enhance and release, and will never restrict or stifle the life they contain. In fact, if the Church is to function as the body of Christ, its structures should function like a skeleton. A body cannot work without its skeleton but the skeleton itself is unseen and unnoticed. The only time it ever gets attention is when it is used for something for which it was never intended, and its bones get damaged and broken. Apply this picture to the Church, and we have to admit that at times it looks like a walking skeleton. At our worst, we can be guilty of exhibiting and parading our structures at the expense of showing the image of Christ to the watching world. Instead of seeing the love of Jesus, they are presented with a lifeless and rigid institution, going through the motions. But the Church should not be a skeleton; it is the living, breathing body of Christ that attracts, engages and heals, and any structure must be careful to reflect and release that life.

Power

Structures have a powerful influence, and the source of that power can either be the key to life or bring the kiss of death. Throughout its history, the Church has wrestled with its desire to follow the Spirit of God, yet it has often succumbed to the spirit of the institution. One of the greatest challenges of change is to relinquish our own hold on power and to seek the Spirit's power instead. When we do, the process of designing structures becomes a paradigm shift in its own right. Instead of relying on the formal and familiar, we launch out in faith and allow the Spirit of God to provide a landing.

Imagine a spider as it spins its web. It begins with an outer framework, but beyond the frame the web can look very fragile and shambolic to begin with. Essentially, the spider throws itself into the air and sees where the wind will take it. Little by little, it builds a matrix of fragile threads, crisscrossing and interconnecting, until an intricate web is created. Both the process and the threads themselves appear fragile and, on their own, pointless. The finished product, however, is functional, strong and beautiful. This is exactly how I imagine the structures that God wants to build in his Church. They, too, will be functional and attractive, but will come into being, at times, through a measure of faith and risk, and will be born out of fragility and weakness. Like the web, they are made up of many tiny threads that join up at many different points, but the finished work is strong, effective and incredibly efficient.

Weaving the web

As the Church navigates its way into the second decade of the 21st century, new threads are appearing but the web is far from finished. There are many examples emerging, however, that begin to show us how it could look.

At the local level, I think of our own most traditional congregation. Earlier, I described how we moved the time of worship to the afternoon to accommodate the needs of elderly members, and how we provided a pick-up bus to enable them to travel. Even so, we were still faced with a slowly dying congregation that would fade away unless it was radically restructured for mission and growth. Choosing the latter option, we took two out of the four services a month, and looked afresh at their 'up, in, out' shape. On the second Sunday, we replaced the worship service with a community meal that had a short act of worship incorporated. Over the months, the congregation on that day has tripled and regularly welcomes and introduces the unchurched to Sunday worship. Meanwhile, the fourth Sunday is now a united ecumenical service, joining together with the local chapels in our community that were also struggling with attendance. Because they were prepared to address the issues of pruning, purpose and power, and to be far more flexible with their structures, this elderly and traditional congregation has found new heart, as well as being blessed with new life and growth.

In its overall ministry, St Mark's has become very intentional about being a mixed economy church, where inherited and emerging forms of church are developed side by side. We think of ourselves not only as a neighbourhood church but as a network church that is weaving together the many contacts, interests and passions that people have beyond the parish. Working with both models, we have developed the language of 'lake and river' to describe our mission. Lakes tend to form in settled places, where they provide an oasis to the life around them. In the same way, a local community church can be an oasis and a source of life to the community it serves. Rivers, on the other hand, flow wherever the ground gives way and the rain may fall. They are still connected to lakes but are constantly moving and changing shape, just as new forms of church move in and through an ever-changing landscape of networks and other cultures. Both approaches are vital in today's world and together they have given St Mark's its latest purpose statement: 'to pioneer a new future in the lake and river church'.

Finally, what might be developing on the regional and national scene? Again, the threads are still emerging, but networks are beginning to appear that increasingly offer a more flexible approach to regional and denominational structures. In my own context, we are appointing pioneer ministers who are gifted and trained for specific kinds of projects, such as church in schools, workplaces or socially deprived areas, or who are specialists in alternative worship, youth church or café church. As a small project is successfully planted in one area, it can then be offered and multiplied in other similar settings. Each project is structured so that it is not only linked to several local churches but operates as a network church in its own right. As these networks develop, a covenant is created with the neighbourhood churches involved, so that church membership itself consists of two or more threads of belonging. This also means that more and more churches begin to develop a 'lake and river' mentality, and can seriously engage with the challenge of changing shape. All of this requires enormous flexibility, of course. It also raises the question of symmetry, the fifth principle for redesigning church.

FIFTH PRINCIPLE: DEVELOPING SPACE

If all of the previous four principles are taken on board, how do we measure things like membership, belonging and commitment? Even if a majority of Christians continue to be members of a single local church, we may increasingly find it difficult to define where and how they fit in. Traditionally, apart from visiting the flock, church leaders have tended to look through the building on a Sunday morning with a 'see who's there' mentality. This has become difficult as attendance has become more erratic, and even home group leaders experience a lack of consistency in terms of attendance. Add to that the possibility that membership and belonging may increasingly be spread across several networks as well as neighbourhoods, and the picture becomes even more messy and blurred. Again, we need to find a new paradigm for helping people understand how and where they belong.

Four spaces of belonging

In the 1960s, a study by Edward T. Hall[8] identified four spaces of human interaction—four areas that people move in and out of as they build relationships. More recently, Joseph R. Myers has developed this idea from a Christian perspective, and talks about the 'four spaces of belonging'—public, social, personal and intimate space, four areas that we all naturally move in and out of in the search for a place to belong.[9] I have found these categories very helpful in reshaping my own understanding of Christian belonging and discipleship. In fact, they translate very simply into the four Cs of community: celebration, cluster, cell and covenant relationships. Together they offer a useful tool that enables church members to think about their spiritual and pastoral diet and reflect on where, when and how they fit into the body of Christ.

Public space: celebration

Public space is where people make connections with each other on a large scale, and where they find belonging through a shared experience. This connection may happen in a football stadium, a theatre or a favourite shopping mall or supermarket. In public space, people have the freedom to remain anonymous without feeling that they are strangers. At the same time, they feel they are a significant part of whatever is happening there and share a sense of belonging with others in that place. In the church setting, we enter public space through the Sunday services and larger congregational gatherings. It is a place where we can connect with each other and God through a shared experience, and yet we can, if we choose, remain anonymous.

In truth, there are many people who attend our church services who will never attend anything else. St Mark's, for instance, is a cell-based church where the majority are involved in small groups, yet there is a significant minority who faithfully come along to Sunday service every single week but never get involved elsewhere. For them, public celebration is not just a place of connection but an opportunity for genuine belonging and community, and their attendance is often more regular than that of many of our cell group members.

Social space: cluster

We move into social space whenever we cluster around a common interest or focus and begin to interact with each other. Typically, we experience social space when we visit our local club or pub, or attend a party or function. In this space, we connect with people on a superficial level by sharing snapshots of ourselves, introducing who we are, what we enjoy and where and how we live. This space is particularly important as a springboard into all the other spaces. It is where we are introduced to new people, ideas and invitations, and is therefore an important space in the context of mission. As we gather with unchurched people around a common sphere of interest, that is where we can most naturally begin to share snapshots of what church is about, who God is and what it means to believe.

Personal space: cell

Personal space happens at the smaller group level, where we develop closer friendships, work with our colleagues, and live alongside our families and neighbours. It is the place where we know each other well and begin to share more privately with people. As Christians, we enter personal space in our cells and small groups, as we reflect together on our faith, share our lives and pray for one another.

Intimate space: covenant relationship

Intimate space is shared with very few people. Apart from our spouse, it may include one or two very close friends, and these are the people who know us as we really are, warts and all. In intimate space, the emphasis is on being 'naked and not ashamed' (see Genesis 2:25), where we feel safe and secure in sharing the naked truth about ourselves. In the Christian community, we experience intimate space through covenant relationships, deeper friendships and accountability groups, and also in the counselling context.

Entering Jesus' space

As we follow Jesus through the Gospels, we see him moving in and out of all four spaces. More important, we see him making significant connections with people in each and every space, never implying that one space is more significant than another. The centurion who asked Jesus to heal his servant, for instance, was not ready to have Jesus share his home but was desperate to be included as a follower in the crowd. Jesus honoured that desire and still blessed him in an intimate way (Matthew 8:5–13). We see Jesus attending weddings, talking to fishermen and visiting people's homes, all the time sharing snapshots of himself and his Father and inviting his audience to follow him more closely. As they did so, he entered the privacy of personal space with the twelve disciples, and then a more intimate space with Peter, James and John. Only these three were allowed to be with him on the mount of transfiguration (Matthew 17:1) and in the garden where he prayed before his arrest (Mark 14:33).

In short, the fullness of life that Jesus offered was encapsulated in the fullness of belonging that he modelled. Not long after he left his disciples, the early Church was living and moving in all four spaces, celebrating its life at every level. Will the Church today continue to follow suit and, if so, how will it best be able to do so in an ever-changing context?

Space to grow

As I've grappled as a pastor with the challenge of change and changing shape, the four spaces have become a very helpful tool in encouraging people to have a healthy spiritual diet, whatever their current life situation. Instead of looking only at Sunday and cell attendance, we now encourage people to look at their diet in general. Using the four spaces, people can begin to measure how and where they belong in the body of Christ. Over a month, for instance, they may attend two out of four services and three out of four cell meetings, meet once with a covenant friend and commit to a monthly 'fresh expression'. They could, of course, do things in a dozen different ways, depending on their circumstances, but the symmetry of celebration, cluster, cell and covenant will help them to find fulfilment, depth and balance in their ongoing search to belong. It will also enable them to move within a more sympathetic church paradigm.

We began this chapter with images of fathers and family, so let's end on the same note. When I spend time with my own family, we sit around and listen to each other's stories. Whether I'm listening to my wife talk about life at school or hearing about the latest movements in the music business or the outrageous things that happen in the worlds of pop and punk, I don't understand a lot about those worlds. But I love to hear about what my family members are doing because I love them, and I want to listen, engage and celebrate their experiences with them. My hope and passion is that the family of God will learn to do the same, and especially as it navigates a course through unfamiliar waters. Whether we choose to sail on the lake of our traditions or swim in the rivers of redesign, we not only share the same living water, but heaven, in the end, will welcome us all into the very same sea. As a friend of mine used to say, 'I hope you're enjoying unity and diversity now, or heaven will be hell for you!'

---- ✢ ----

MEETING THE CHALLENGE

Doing it with style

- How many different styles and how much variety is there in your church's ministry?
- How intentional is your church in encouraging a variety of styles?

- What, if anything, would you like to introduce to the mix, and what would it look like?
- Are there other churches or networks with which you can collaborate to provide more variety?

Dealing with size

- Does your church have a positive or negative attitude to the idea of 'small'?
- Can you identify possible projects that could be grown from the starting point of two or three people?
- Does your church have a healthy mixture of smaller and larger gatherings, or does the Sunday service model still dominate?

Drawing the shape

- Using the model of 'up, in, out', where is your church strongest and weakest at the moment?
- Think of the particular ministry or small group that you are a part of, and apply the same question to it.
- If you are already developing a 'fresh expression', is it a fresh expression of worship, community or mission, or all three (in other words, a full fresh expression of church)?

Designing structures

- Are the structures of your church rigid and permanent or soft and flexible?
- Are there structures stopping your church from considering something new? If so, how can they be changed?

- Do you need to prune anything in the life of the church, in order to plant something new?
- Does your church look more like the burning building, the skeleton or the web?
- How do you feel about the concept of a mixed economy church? What would it look like in your context?

Developing space

- Does your church provide a balanced diet in the way it enables people to belong?
- How would it score in providing public, social, personal and intimate spaces for people to connect?
- Taking the symmetry of all four spaces, how does your own diet look at the moment? Are there elements missing that you would like to add?

Chapter Seven

RE-IMAGINING LEADERSHIP

To put it bluntly: the whole leadership thing is a demented concept. Leaders are neither born nor made. Leaders are summoned. They are called into existence by circumstances, and those who rise to the occasion are leaders.
LEONARD SWEET[1]

Sweet's provocative take on leadership resonates loudly in my own experience. Like him, I've seen a smattering of unusually gifted characters who would naturally excel as leaders in any context, and I've also seen those who are the fruit of effective training and development programmes. Above all, I've been amazed by the way God has taken raw and fragile material and simply anointed people for a season of leadership. I should mention here that the parish of Haydock is not the most fertile ground for finding ready-grown leaders. Not many come with impressive CVs of academic success, or directorial or management prowess, or even a great measure of confidence. Over the years, however, God has summoned the willing, and a very ordinary community has at times seen extraordinary blessing in its ministry and mission. But why should that surprise us? The Bible and the history of the Church are littered with examples of God taking hold of untested, untrained and seemingly unsuitable people; while the world has continued to grow and groom its Sauls, the Davids have been summoned by divine appointment.

I have always liked the definition of a leader as 'a person with a magnet in his heart and a compass in his head'. In other words, it is all about vision and the ability to sense where the Spirit of God is moving. Unfortunately, not every person with the gift of leadership has the gift of vision. When Moses sent twelve spies to explore the land of Canaan, we're told that 'all of them were leaders' (Numbers 13:3), but only Joshua and Caleb came back with the vision of a new future. While they saw a land that was 'exceedingly good' (14:7), flowing with milk and honey and fruit, the other ten saw only powerful giants and fortified cities. Their negative influence led to weeping, grumbling and talk of violent rebellion among the people, followed by God's declaration that 'not one of you will enter the land' (v. 30).

SEEING IS BELIEVING

In the normal scheme of things, most people, like the disciple Thomas (John 20:25), want to experience something tangible before they'll believe, especially when it comes to vision. On the other hand, those who are summoned by God to lead, and especially those who are called to pioneer, do so because they're willing to see things, particularly the future, through the lens of faith. For them, seeing really is believing, but it's a seeing with the heart that comes long before a physical view.

Joshua was one such pioneer and we can learn much from him about what it means to be a leader of change, crossing over from a desert past into a new and abundant future. Indeed, when the time came for him to take the lead and enter Canaan, his very first action was to learn from the previous disastrous episode. This time, he deliberately sent only two spies to look over the land, and they are not even described as leaders (Joshua 2:1). You can imagine his strategy as he deliberately shunned all the appointed leaders, born or made, from the twelve tribes of Israel and said to himself, 'Never mind the twelve; two will do. Two men who will move into Canaan and won't be intimidated by the size of the task or the scale of the enemy, and who'll come back with an accurate report and a healthy vision—that's what we need!' And that's what we need in the Church today as it journeys into the future.

Seeing the believing

In 1777 John Wesley wrote in a letter, 'Give me one hundred preachers who fear nothing but sin and desire nothing but God, and I care not a straw whether they be clergy or lay, such alone will shake the gates of hell and set up the kingdom of heaven upon earth.' Wesley knew that our strength is never in our numbers or our name, or even our new ideas, but in our knowledge of God. In fact, God can use two vision-fuelled believers far more than he can ever use 200 faithless and negative church members. Once again, it is the mustard seed principle at work, and it provides sound guidance when we are looking out for the 'summoned'. As we survey our Christian community, where are the mustard seeds of faith and vision to be found? Where are the seeds of grace beginning to grow and flourish? Who has an increasingly mission-shaped heart and a passion to see God move in the networks they inhabit? This is not about hot air and cool ideas, but about those who are focused on God. Not only will they have all the hallmarks of honesty, humility, hunger, hurt, harmony and hope that we looked at in Chapter One, but they will be those who can look towards the future and, like Joshua and Caleb, see as God sees.

Believing what we see

How do we know that what such leaders see is truly of God? All of us are tinged with our own prejudice and preferences, so we are bound sometimes to see the same picture from very different perspectives. It is rather like the joke about the Englishman, Frenchman and Russian who are viewing a painting of Adam and Eve in the Garden of Eden.

'Look at their quiet calm and reserve,' mused the Englishman. 'They must be British.'

'Nonsense,' said the Frenchman. 'They are naked and so beautiful. Clearly they are French.'

But the Russian complained, 'They have no clothes or shelter and only an apple to eat, and they're being told this is paradise! They have to be Russian.'

We are all coloured by our background but, drawing on the principles we have talked about so far, I think that is precisely the point. God uses our background to shape us in specific ways. When he adds to that both his leadership summons and the anointing of his Spirit, we are equipped to pioneer in the places he has already put us.

When we first started to move out of our church building into the networks, I soon learned a humbling lesson about my own leadership. I realized that the gifts, skills and instincts that I exercised within my church's culture could not easily be transferred into other cultures. For instance, I discovered that the person best suited to the rough-and-tumble banter of our local pub was not the vicar but rather a brash and blunt Christian called Brian, who understood and fitted into that community in a way that I never could. 'Brash and blunt' he may have appeared on the outside, but Brian had long had a gracious servant heart, as well as a vision for serving the disadvantaged. Ironically, Brian had failed to be selected for ordination to the priesthood, and yet he epitomizes the kind of pioneer who can walk into his local pub and proclaim with authority and bluntness, 'The kingdom of God is near you!'

Once again, we are thinking and moving in a new paradigm here, for what is being described has little connection with formal theological college training or the familiar trappings of pulpits and dog collars. Of course, traditional models of ministry and leadership are as essential as ever, but a change in the shape of church will also require a new shape of leader alongside the old. Let's take a closer look at how a changing world will require a changing leadership, and what might emerge as a result. To do that, we will explore a range of images that can help us to visualize a new paradigm for leadership.

FROM RESTRUCTURING TO REIMAGINING

The first image was given to me in conversation by George Lings, who compares the Church to a swimming pool with a diving board. He suggests that all our efforts to do church and mission effectively are like standing someone on the board and teaching them how to perform a perfect dive into the pool. The problem, he says, is that doing mission today is a completely different sport, and it's not a diving board we need but a surf board. We need to understand that pioneering happens in a completely different environment, down on the beach. It is not about swimming in the relative safety of the pool but about trying to catch and ride the waves in an unpredictable ocean. As such, it is not only exciting and slightly nerve-racking, but it can take us just about anywhere as we try to respond to the movement of God in unpredictable and unfamiliar waters. Developing the image further, George said to me, 'Do you know what scares me to death? It's that the Church has suddenly discovered surfing, and it's saying, "This is exciting; now how can we build a wave machine to put inside the pool?"'

This image alone encapsulates the message of the last three chapters. We need as many surfers as divers in the kingdom of God, people who not only live on the beach and know the ocean but who can ride the wave of mission opportunities that unchurched communities bring. In this context, Brian is a surfer. With his own particular cultural branding and his caring, serving and gathering skills, he can ride skilfully over the waves of banter and bad news that he encounters on a daily basis. Meanwhile, Brian himself is at home both in the pool and in the ocean. Because of this, some of his pub contacts will accompany him to church on a Sunday morning, as well as belonging to the fresh expression of church that he and others are building. When it came to baptizing four people from the same family, they were given the choice of being baptized in the pub or the church. Two chose the church, while the other two opted for the pub, the place where they felt at home, where they had gathered with believers and come to faith. Pioneers can be surfers or divers but they don't build wave machines in pools.

FROM ATTRACTING TO ATTACHING

The second image is borrowed from a book by John Dominic Crossan, called *The Dark Interval*. In it, he pictures a sea that is covered with people living on rafts. Once upon a time, they were guided back to land by a lighthouse and its keeper on the rock, but now everything has changed: 'There is no lighthouse keeper, there is no lighthouse. There is no dry land. There are only people living on rafts made from their own imaginations. And there is the sea.'[2]

Just as those people could no longer see the lighthouse or the keeper, so our world and its perception of the Church have changed. For centuries, people were guided toward the safety and stability of a strong and recognized Church that not only offered the security of faith, hope and belonging, but was firmly built on a familiar and immovable landscape of culture and tradition. Today, however, the landscape itself has shifted and, in places, disappeared. In a vastly changed and uncertain world, many people are now attempting to live on rafts of their own making. They sail through life precariously on a restless sea of doubts, hunches and uncertainties, free to float wherever they wish but fragile, insecure and disoriented as a result.

Many churches today still see themselves as lighthouses, offering guidance aimed at attracting people back to a solid faith. It's worth remembering, however, that lighthouses themselves have the paradoxical role of both attracting and warning ships off. In other words, they attract attention and guide people towards safety, but, if you try and anchor near one, you're in danger of being shipwrecked. The Church exists to offer light and guidance but its ultimate aim is to guide people to the haven of authentic community. If it fails to do that, believers can end up shipwrecked on the rocks of a deadly institutionalism.

Returning to Crossan's picture, however, the focus is on all the people who can no longer even recognize what a lighthouse is through the fog of our culture, and for whom the landscape itself has changed or even disappeared. As they cling to their flimsy rafts, it is up to the pioneers to attach themselves to the little groups and networks that people float around in, and to offer them light and community there.

My friend Phil is a pioneer of this kind. Attaching himself to the 'raft' of Rugby League, he's spent the last few years serving one of the professional teams, befriending, bag carrying and providing pastoral and practical backup to the players, trainers and their families. He's never asked them to come to church or an evangelistic event, even though he himself is a leader and organizer in both such contexts. Instead, he's done no more than attach himself to the raft. From there, he not only shares their fragile, unstable world, but he looks out from the raft as they do and he begins to see the fog that stops the others from ever seeing a lighthouse. He travels with them to matches, Sunday by Sunday, realizing that the concept of Sunday church attendance would never enter their heads, but he also invites them to a weekly evening get-together in his home. There they share a meal, watch and discuss a film, and then engage in worship and prayer. Little by little, the raft has become more and more secure and strong, as whole families have started to come to faith and discover a new kind of community.

Fresh expressions of church are often built on the rafts of such small, drifting and often frail communities, and there are thousands upon thousands of them out there. One day, the people on those rafts may see a lighthouse again and find new shores, but the Church of the 21st century will also need to be built on rafts and led by pioneers.

FROM RETAINING TO RELEASING AND REPRODUCING

The third image comes from a book on 'the unstoppable power of leaderless organizations'.[3] In this picture, we imagine a starfish and a spider. Take hold of the spider, cut off its head, and the spider will die. A starfish, however, can have its legs cut off, and not only will the starfish grow new legs but the legs themselves will grow into starfish.

The book explores the demise of huge centralized organizations in a globalized world, and the astonishing energy, power and growth that has been released through those that have chosen to decentralize. The Internet revolution, for instance, has empowered the masses to contribute in creating and reproducing products. Wikipedia, eBay, Skype and Apple are all now household names and have helped to revolutionize the way we communicate and consume. Even so, as recently as 1995, a group of French investors was brought together to discuss the funding of Internet providers and their overriding question was, 'Who is the president of the Internet'? However that question was addressed, they could not understand the concept of a network of networks that had no president but could still connect communities in a radically new and different way. Since then, of course, the winds of change have rapidly blown aside that ignorance and the revolution has taken hold.

Meanwhile, equally startling stories are beginning to emerge from more traditional organizations. General Motors, for example, employed Peter Drucker in the 1940s to explore and explain the secret of their success and to make proposals for their future. A year later, he published his findings, suggesting that the company should loosen its structures and decentralize in order to release more energy and growth. The company was infuriated by his report and rejected it outright. Drucker, meanwhile, took his theories to Japan, where the Japanese car industry embraced them enthusiastically. Years later, after ongoing and increasing productivity, Toyota was invited to America to help an ailing General Motors, and within three years the results there were staggering.

You may remember the old song by Sting, 'If you love somebody set them free'. The problem in all walks of life, however, is that leaders love to lead so much that they often find it very difficult to let go and let others take the field. In effect, they love what they're building, but not enough to set it free. Church leaders are no different, and sometimes it can take many years before a professional minister begins to delegate and share his or her ministry with others. Whole books have been written on the benefits and importance of a shared leadership, but, on a personal level, it has been one of the major keys to releasing growth in our church. It began at St Mark's with a single team who, between them, served and facilitated the various ministries. It continued to grow as the building and ministries were reordered through the introduction of several teams. After that, the influence of cell church led to an even broader restructuring and releasing of leaders, until the team of ten had grown to a community of 100. Since then, releasing has taken on a new form as the church has come to recognize the new shape of leader that God is currently raising up to minister in fresh contexts.

Releasing, of course, involves risk-taking, but in the spiritual realm it unleashes life and allows grace a freer reign. A slogan I've adopted and found helpful is 'high accountability, low control'. In other words, releasing is not about putting things 'out of sight and out of mind', but about building deep and trusting relationships, where contact is frequent, communication is strong, and coaching is applied and personal.

FROM ORCHESTRATING TO IMPROVISING

The fourth image is of orchestras and jazz bands, and is developed in a book entitled *All That Jazz* by Fred Drummond.[4] Orchestras, of course, are strongly structured and tightly led. Every person plays exactly what they are asked to play, and the overall piece is pulled together and interpreted by the conductor. In general, well-led churches have traditionally been handled like orchestras, where the leadership has a clear plan, a specific list of projects and ministries, and a very fixed idea of how to conduct the congregation.

Orchestras can produce moving and beautiful music, but so can jazz bands. In a band, everybody is also playing in the same key and off the same page, but there the similarity ends. Jazz bands are made up of people with a very different gift mix and a diversity of talents, who all agree to improvise and see where the music takes them. On the surface, they may appear to look and sound random, but as they focus on listening and interacting with each other, and as they hone and build a mutual trust and understanding, the music miraculously comes together. The pooling of resources and the playing with possibilities produces, in the end, a finely tuned piece of music.

Missional communities operate like jazz bands. They rarely have a qualified conductor, but do attract extraordinary gifts in connecting with a particular culture. As I've mentioned, the café church I'm involved in is led by a group of very artistic people, whose improvisation of skills has led to an equally artistic expression of church. At the other end of the spectrum, the efficient environment of the police community has produced an equally well-attuned leadership, with impressive networking, management and communication skills. The Christian community there has been speedily and well shaped around its supportive cell structures. Famlegh First, meanwhile, is not only child-centred but, with the combined skills of teachers, parents and grandparents, has a natural and specific focus on parenting and helping families to engage with each other. In every case, there is an improvisation of skills that fits the context, along with a range of spiritual gifts, and together they provide the foundation for a kind of leadership that is not only creative and flexible but also well tuned to both church and culture.

FROM CONTROLLING TO CULTIVATING

The fifth and final picture invites us to imagine half a dozen contrasting types of leader. In an article entitled 'A new kind of leader',[5] Tim Elmore charts the way the world has changed over the last 50 years or so in the way that it views leadership. It is a broad and generalized picture but Elmore argues that, in the 1950s, the dominant picture was of the military commander, very top-down and controlling. During this phase, leaders enjoyed directing events from their position of authority, and people in every context (including churches) would tend to do whatever they were told. As society changed, the late 1960s and '70s produced the Chief Executive Officer. As people grew increasingly disillusioned with the failings and fallibilities of authority, they demanded to be motivated rather than ordered by their leaders, and insisted on being sold a vision before they would choose to submit. This was followed in the 1980s by the Entrepreneur, and the emphasis swung toward creativity and innovation, and leading from the front by example. The 1990s then engaged with the newly evolved Generation X, those born after 1964, for whom relationships and team work counted more than bosses, so an emphasis on coaching and team building developed.

As the new century has progressed, all the previous leadership models are still around and continue to work, their effectiveness depending on generation, temperament and personality, but two new leadership types have now begun to appear. Elmore identifies these as 'the poet' and 'the gardener'. Poets do not assume that they have all the answers but surround themselves with a team of other leaders. Together, they listen to their culture and context, and the poet-leader's role is to summarize and synthesize the ideas that emerge and then galvanize the team into action. In confusing and fast-changing contexts, poet-leaders give language to the ideas and imaginations of others, and enable others to feel part of the creative leadership process. Gardeners, similarly, create the kind of environment where creativity can happen, where people can thrive and grow. Very simply, a gardener cultivates the soil and pulls the weeds, enabling a garden of flourishing plants to appear. The gardener leader focuses on developing both the place and the people to produce the best possible environment for healthy, vigorous growth. In both these models, the emphasis is on connection, community and a shared creativity that empowers people to feel part of the leadership process.

In my own leadership journey, I can see traces of all the leadership styles that Elmore describes, but the 'poet–gardener' model has been critical in planting new forms of church. To do this effectively, I have needed to recognize that many of the contexts and cultures I enter as a leader are foreign to me. When I walk into police headquarters or my wife's staff room or the local Working Men's Club, a part of me feels uncomfortable and ill at ease. I need the guidance of those who live and belong in those environments to understand their values and rules, behaviour and banter. Perhaps this is why the Church at times has been slow to move into these places in mission. If the initiative is solely in the hands of the vicar, then my church is unlikely to engage in very many contexts, simply because its leadership will naturally only be at home in one or two outside its own church setting. That is why my own leadership style looks very different now in equipping others to lead. As a 'poet/gardener', my primary role is to gather a team of people who live and move in a particular culture and equip them to develop church in those places. To do this, I listen to their stories, hear their ideas and encourage their passion, then galvanize and inspire them into building something that is appropriate and relevant in their particular setting. Very simply, my role is to create an environment where indigenous leadership can blossom and grow, and a place where passion can be translated into a workable vision.

As we grapple with the challenge of shaping change and changing the shape of church, poets and gardeners are increasingly the kind of leaders we need to enable fresh thinking, release new initiative and equip the church to dream. In fact, their role is vital in focusing on the future and helping the church to appreciate what the future requires. Because change is a process, for instance, it is all too easy to look at a work in progress and fail to appreciate its worth. One of the more hurtful comments that pioneers receive is that 'nobody has a clue what they're doing'. Because a fresh expression of church is unfamiliar and unfinished, people can easily assume that it isn't 'proper church'. Poets and gardeners, however, create an environment where change is encouraged, embraced and understood, and they can also develop a language that enables people to grasp and engage with what is happening.

For instance, sometimes I find I have to defend the style and content of teaching to be found in fresh expressions of church. A visiting church leader may hear a brief, informal talk being delivered to an unchurched audience and compare it unfavourably to traditional expository preaching. Here, the poet leader's role is to point out the context, explain the culture and emphasize the importance of only offering 'snapshots' of faith to an unconverted and uninitiated audience. Meanwhile, they may also use the language of 'up, in, out' as a helpful means of enabling people to make a balanced appraisal of the church they see emerging. New forms of church require new tools to give them shape but also a new language to give people an understanding of what is being shaped.

So today's pioneer leaders are like surfers, starfish, gardeners and poets, who live on rafts and play in jazz bands. No wonder they're often seen as mavericks and mischief makers, especially by those suspicious of change. When pioneers are summoned by God, however, he shapes them in creative and imaginative ways and then calls them to reshape church until it becomes more mission-shaped.

PORTRAITS OF A PIONEER

Turning back to the Bible, the account of Joshua's pioneer leadership gives us an inspiring model to follow. From the outset, we see that his story is one of constant movement, from the old to the new, from one generation to the next, from the land of slavery to the land of promise, from desert land to a land of abundance. Joshua was a champion of change but he was also a child of God who walked a path of meekness in following God's call. Anyone who aspires to be a pioneer and leader of change will do well to follow his example, and should take note of what, in particular, a pioneer is actually called to do.

A call to serve and sacrifice

If you had to give Joshua a title, what would it be? Would you label him as a famous general, a great leader or a heroic pioneer? The Bible describes him simply as 'Moses' aide'. Not only that, but he'd spent 40 years in the wilderness helping Moses, and before that would have endured slavery, humiliation and oppression at the hands of the Egyptians. Joshua may have made a sudden and dramatic mark as a pioneer leader but it was preceded by a long, slow and often painful development process. Step by step, God had prepared him for a unique ministry and, by the time Moses died and Joshua took his place, Deuteronomy 34:9 singles out one particular quality that qualified him for the task ahead: 'Joshua son of Nun was filled with the spirit of wisdom.'

People who are pioneers in church ministry need huge amounts of wisdom, and it's not a quality that appears overnight. It comes with a learning heart, the attitude of a servant and a measure of experience. A summons to the limelight of leadership may come suddenly but the preparation normally takes place slowly, almost imperceptibly, in hidden and sometimes difficult places. This point is an important one because pioneers, by nature, can be restless and impatient and will instinctively want to be at the head of the queue when any assignments to do with change are being handed out.

A call to leave the past behind

Shortly after I arrived in Haydock as the new vicar, I went to a leadership seminar based on the book of Joshua. I can't remember much about that day, apart from one talk that was built around five words from Joshua 1:2: 'Moses my servant is dead.' The speaker explained that there comes a time when the ministries of the past should be given a decent burial, so that the ministries and ministers of the present can enter into their own inheritance. He drew attention to the astonishing testimony of Moses and all that was accomplished in his lifetime, as a reluctant leader led a rebellious people to release from slavery. But then, he said, a new phase in God's plan needed a new generation with new gifts and new insight, along with a fresh vision for entering into a whole new inheritance. Putting it bluntly, we cannot have Canaan and keep Moses, and, before we can receive anything new with open hands, we have to let go of something else.

At the time, I can remember feeling haunted by the ghosts of the past and paralyzed by all the sacred cows that seemed to block a path to the future. The message to move on was clear and un-compromising, however, and I knew that the first step was to share it with the church and invite them to journey with me. Since then, we have learnt together to honour, harness and heal the past (as discussed earlier in the book), and never to ignore or negate it. Crucially, we have learned when it's time to bury the past and build on it. To be a pioneer is not to be an undertaker but it is to be a pastor who leads the tributes and allows the grieving, and then enables the family to move on.

A call to go the whole way

Whenever God gives a command in scripture, he always accompanies it with a promise. Joshua receives four promises at the beginning of the book that bears his name. He is promised provision (1:3–4), protection (v. 5), presence (v. 5) and prosperity (v. 8). But the com-mand also comes without compromise: 'Make sure that you obey the whole Law that my servant Moses gave you. Do not neglect any part of it and you will succeed wherever you go' (v. 7, GNB).

Joshua here is encouraged to go the whole way in order to receive the whole blessing. Sadly, the reason why many of us are only half happy, half the time, is often that we have gone only halfway in our discipleship. If our worship is half-hearted, only half of our heart is spiritually alive. If our commitment to community is only half-baked and our relationship difficulties half-resolved, then we feel only half-loved. If we feed from God's word for only half a minute now and then, we end up only half understanding his plan for our lives. But the same principle applies in leadership: once the call is clear to pioneer, move on and face the challenge of change, to do things by halves is not an option. Tragically, the Church is strewn with half-planned, half-hearted and half-finished projects that can leave us in a worse position than when we first started. Changes in the church's life that are only half agreed lead to anger and division. Half-planned projects fall apart and fall on deaf ears, while half a budget will often produce half a job well done. Wherever God is calling us to move in the realm of change, whether it be near or far, his call is always to go the whole way.

Another challenging 'half' word is the word 'halfway'. Many of the Bible's pioneers stumbled at the halfway stage. The book of Nehemiah offers perhaps the most memorable example. As the walls of Jerusalem were being rebuilt, the people's eagerness to work was slowly overtaken by tiredness. As the wall reached half its height, one by one they began to complain: 'The strength of the labourers is giving out, and there is so much rubble that we cannot rebuild the wall' (Nehemiah 4:10). You can begin with lots of energy, enthusiasm and drive, and you can also end with the excitement of seeing the goal in sight, but the halfway point is always hardest. If you decide to decorate your house, as you reach the halfway stage the empty walls, tins of paint and rolls of wallpaper are still sitting there accusing you, even though you have been hard at work for weeks. Or if you decide to climb a mountain, as you reach the ridge that you thought was near the top, you find another couple of ridges on the other side. Even Joshua, with his endless drive and energy, had to face the halfway challenge. Joshua 12 lists a huge catalogue of defeated kings, but it is immediately followed by the observation, 'When Joshua was old and well advanced in years, the Lord said to him, "You are very old, and there are still very large areas of land to be taken over"' (13:1).

Change can seem demoralizingly slow at times, and the pioneer must learn the art of patience as well as persistence, never losing the will to go the distance or the call to go the whole way.

A call to walk ahead

One of the more powerful images of pioneering leadership from Joshua's story is that of the priests who carried the ark of the covenant across the river Jordan. In Joshua 3:6, they are instructed to 'pass on ahead of the people', and there has to be a 1000-yard gap between them and those who followed. This also reminds me of the moment in Gethsemane when Jesus went 'a little farther' (Matthew 26:39), leaving his disciples to drift off to sleep while he began to embrace his ultimate call. Leaders, and especially pioneers, will tend to find themselves out front and on their own. Leaders of change, in particular, will often have to live alone with their vision before others begin to embrace it. Sometimes it is a gap of days or weeks, but there can often be a gap of months or even years before others catch up and catch on.

The implications of this are twofold. First of all, it is important to remember that we can only take people as far as we ourselves have been. For instance, it is no good talking about reordering buildings for better worship, community and mission unless we have already reordered our focus and are beginning to model what the future could look like through the ministries we've already introduced. And it is no use suggesting that we engage with the world in fresh and relevant ways unless we can illustrate it through the personal image that we ourselves present of priesthood and Christian ministry. Change begins in the leader, and the leader always walks ahead.

The second implication is loneliness. If you are walking ahead on your own, then many people will never see what you see, feel what you feel and struggle where you will inevitably struggle. Nor will they need to have quite the same level of faith that you needed or face some of the agonies and challenges that you had to face. Somebody described being a leader as being an arrowhead. It means that everything coming behind you will never have to penetrate at the same level that you did in order to get a breakthrough. This is why the sharing of leadership is essential in facing the challenge of pioneering change. In the crossing of the Jordan, the heroic Joshua wasn't on his own at the front, but there was a whole group of Levites bearing the symbol of God's presence.

A call to walk alongside

The call to walk ahead may involve loneliness but it is never a call to isolation. Pioneering may begin at the front but it moves with those at the back as well, and especially with those who straggle or come to a stop. The Jordan river crossing involved the priests moving ahead, but then they stood in the middle of the river until the 'whole nation' had completed the crossing, including the stragglers (Joshua 3:17). In any change process, there will always be some who lag behind the rest. The temptation for pioneers will often be to move on and leave them behind, even failing to notice their absence, but the Church of God is a single body that, whenever possible, should move as one.

Earlier in the story, we read that the tribes of Reuben and Gad decided to stay on the eastern side of the Jordan, arguing that they didn't need to possess Canaan. Long before the Jordan crossing, they had found a lovely piece of land that had quite enough milk and honey for them, without the need to go any further or conquer another seven nations (Numbers 32). Moses' answer was to reprimand them, warning that their decision would cause Israel to lose heart (vv. 6–15). He insisted that they cross over the Jordan with everyone else, to help the other tribes possess the land. The Reubenites were a strong tribe who carried much influence, and in the book of Joshua we see them fulfilling their obligation before eventually returning to enjoy the streams of Gilead (22:9). Again, this reminds us of the importance of investing in the whole body of Christ and insisting that, where possible, every member plays a vital part in shaping the future. It may well be that the majority is not directly involved in church planting or projects to do with change, but they can still support with their encouragement, finance, understanding and prayer. Pioneers need to work to ensure that those at the front connect with those who remain at the rear, and find ways of uniting everyone around the common cause.

We see a further aspect of this in Joshua 18, as Joshua addresses the fact that seven tribes have still not possessed their inheritance but have come to a halt along the way. The promised inheritance was breathtakingly rich, as we read in Moses' blessing on the tribes in Deuteronomy 33. Issachar, for instance, had been told that they would 'feast on the abundance of the seas' and 'on the treasures hidden in the sand' (v. 19), while the descendants of Joseph would enjoy 'the choicest gifts of the ancient mountains and the fruitfulness of the everlasting hills' (v. 15). Astonishingly, after 17 chapters of battles and conquests, Joshua still has to say to the seven remaining tribes, 'How long will you wait before you begin to take possession of the land that the Lord, the God of your fathers, has given you?' (Joshua 18:3).

There is a huge difference between inheritance and possession, and pioneers are called not only to embrace and enjoy the fruits of change, but also to encourage and empower others to do the same. A church building, for example, may be beautifully and imaginatively reordered but, unless it is then used to its maximum potential, the vision has been wasted. In fact, in every major project that I've seen completed, I've been delighted to discover a whole range of additional benefits that I'd not seen at the beginning. The vision of inheritance and possession that God promises us is an astonishing one, but pioneer leaders are called to keep reminding those beside whom they walk, that they must work to take full possession of the promised inheritance.

A call to pass on and pick up the mantle

The final chapter in Joshua's life offers a poignant warning for today's leaders, to remember to train up tomorrow's leaders too. As Joshua dies, we read that 'Israel served the Lord throughout the lifetime... of the elders who outlived him and who had experienced everything the Lord had done for Israel' (24:31). The point is repeated in Judges 2, but it is followed immediately by the tragic truth that 'after that whole generation had been gathered to their fathers, another generation grew up, who knew neither the Lord nor what he had done for Israel' (v. 10). The challenge of change includes a call to pass on everything we have ever learnt to the next generation. Although we can only imagine the specific challenges they will have to face, we do understand both the call and the challenging path that pioneers have to travel, and we negate our own anointing if we do not try to secure the future by passing the mantle to others.

Perhaps the most dramatic example of mantle-passing occurred when Elisha asked Elijah for a double portion of his spirit. Elijah replied, 'You have asked a difficult thing... yet if you see me when I am taken from you, it will be yours' (2 Kings 2:10). In other words, vision is again the key to receiving the summons. Elijah was saying that if Elisha could see as he was able to see, and receive the very same vision for himself, then the anointing and the mantle would be his too.

As we look to the future, the Church will need leaders of every shape and size to meet the challenge of a changing world. The many images described in this chapter reflect the fact that there is no such thing as 'one size fits all' when it comes to Christian leadership. This is why church leaders must have the grace and vision to release many others into ministry, and especially those with a pioneer call. We may not be able to train and resource them all ourselves (and we may not need to), but we can release and enable, encourage and bless. As we do, let's learn to follow the rhythm of Jesus, who sends his disciples 'ahead of him' in mission (Luke 10:1), and then watches for and welcomes their return. And when we see them return 'with joy' (v 17) and begin to tell us their pioneer stories, we too will be able to say with conviction, 'Blessed are the eyes that see what you see' (v. 23).

---- ✠ ----

MEETING THE CHALLENGE

From restructuring to reimagining

- Are you more at home in the swimming pool or the ocean?
- Think about the mission-shaped projects that your church is currently involved in. Do they look more like a wave machine or a surfboard on the ocean?
- Who are the divers and surfers in your church?

From attracting to attaching

- What percentage of your church's mission is about attracting people, and in what ways and in which places is it attaching itself to the rafts and networks that surround your church?
- Who are the potential pioneers, some of whom may already be at work?

From retaining to releasing and reproducing

- Is there a strong commitment to shared ministry in your church?
- How are people released into ministry and leadership?
- How centralized is the leadership?
- To what extent does it take risks in releasing people?

From orchestrating to improvising

- Does the leadership in your church feel more like an orchestra or a jazz band?
- How do you encourage people to improvise and pool their gifts?
- Is your church open to experimentation when it comes to leadership roles and structures?

From controlling to cultivating

- Taking the image of generals, CEOs, entrepreneurs, coaches, poets and gardeners, what style of leadership, if any, dominates in your church?
- What styles of leadership would you like to see more of, and why?

Portraits of a pioneer

- Pioneers are called to serve and sacrifice, leave the past behind, go the whole way, walk ahead and walk alongside, and eventually pass on that calling. Which of these challenges you in your own ministry?
- Which call, in particular, challenges your church leadership as a whole?

Chapter Eight

ALL THINGS NEW!

To myself I seem to have been only like a boy playing on the sea-shore, and diverting myself in now and then finding a smoother pebble or a prettier shell than ordinary, whilst the great ocean of truth lay all undiscovered before me.

SIR ISAAC NEWTON (1642–1727)

These words make me feel small in a very helpful way. They remind me that nobody in the world or the Church has a monopoly on the truth, and that Jesus favours the attitude and approach of 'little children' in kingdom matters (Matthew 18:3). They also remind me that both the most valued traditions and the most innovative changes are like mere shells and pebbles in the purposes of God, and that only heaven will reveal the true picture.

LOOKING FOR HEAVEN

The book of Revelation is particularly inspirational for pioneers of change. Not only does it draw back the curtains of history and reveal the endless movements of a God who is 'making everything new' (Revelation 21:5), but it also shows us where change is ultimately leading. It reminds us that every God-inspired change brings us one step closer to heaven. C.S. Lewis summed it up beautifully in his final Narnian novel, *The Last Battle*, when he wrote:

It was the Unicorn who summed up what everyone was feeling. He stamped his right fore-hoof on the ground and neighed, and then cried:

'I have come home at last! This is my real country! I belong here. This is the land I have been looking for all my life, though I never knew it till now. The reason why we loved the old Narnia is that it sometimes looked a little like this.'[1]

As the Church moves on, every movement for change is simply an expression of longing and looking for heaven and all that it holds. Whenever that is divinely inspired, it not only brings encouragement and joy but it offers, in a real sense, a taste of heaven. Breakthroughs in our worship inspire us to worship more. Transformations in people inspire us to love more, while transformations in our buildings can encourage us to engage and belong more, embracing more ministries and releasing more gifts.

We have seen the importance of paradigm shift, but the greatest shift of all is to see all this change in the light of eternity. I wonder how much we would wrestle with and resist the changes we see around us if we could only see them from heaven's perspective. If I wanted to invest my money in a company and discovered that it was soon to be liquidated, I would be very foolish to invest any of my money there. Yet some of us invest so much of our energy and anxiety into preserving churches that are essentially transient, impermanent and destined for the ultimate change. That is not to say that we shouldn't love them as passionately and unconditionally as Jesus does, but we do it in the context of revelation, the rock-solid certainty that 'we will all be changed', and that 'flesh and blood cannot inherit the kingdom of God' (1 Corinthians 15:50–51). That is why the church in this life must always see itself in the context of the eternal Church, and aspire to prepare and shape itself for heaven. So let's end with a look at the final pages of scripture and four images of heaven to spur us on and inspire us in the challenge of change.

A new universe

Then I saw a new heaven and a new earth, for the first heaven and the first earth had passed away, and there was no longer any sea... He who was seated on the throne said, 'I am making everything new!' (Revelation 21:1, 5).

In Revelation, the sea is a symbol of fear and of the unknown, the same kind of fear that often paralyses a church when it's faced with the possibility of radical change. Here, the fear has gone, but we see change on a universal scale. Not only are we presented with a new earth, but the heavens themselves are recreated by an extravagant God. Of course, trying to explain what heaven will be like could be compared to trying to explain to an unborn child what it will be like to walk, run, laugh, dance and play in the world. In a similar way, the full reality and glory of heaven lie way beyond our present experience. At the moment, in comparison to many animals, you and I are almost blind, deaf and dumb. In our hearing, we are limited to a tiny part of the whole spectrum of sound, yet we can still hear beautiful music. Imagine, then, what it will be like when our ears are really opened and we hear the sounds of heaven! Again, compared to some birds that have telescopic or microscopic sight, you and I are almost blind, but in heaven we will have incredible vision. I could go on, but the point here is not only that God has not finished with us, but that the final product will be infinitely superior: we will be truly transformed. God loves change: he plans for it, pursues it and delivers it on a mind-blowing scale. And once that sea of fear and of the unknown is removed, we will be able to share his perspective.

'No eye has seen, no ear has heard, no mind has conceived what God has prepared for those who love him' (1 Corinthians 2:9). It is so difficult for our finite minds to absorb all this that our natural instinct is to take everything that God has given us so far and to secure it from human tampering. We do this because we cannot grasp that, in God's economy, grace and abundance go on increasing in new and ever more creative ways. David Watson explained the dilemma:

You could sketch a fairly accurate picture of the history of the Church like this: God gives a wonderful fresh breath of Holy Spirit life (at the Day of Pentecost and at various revivals of the Church down the centuries) and man comes along and says, 'That is wonderful! Now let's set up a Church Preservation Society!' Therefore man begins to work out a new denomination, a new church, a new fellowship, a new structure, a new organization, new rules and regulations, new patterns of activities—and the Holy Spirit quietly makes his departure. Does then this great organization collapse over-night? Not a bit of it! It goes on year after year, maybe century after century: the world's tragic counterfeit of the real thing.[2]

We need to remember that the 'real thing' is still a work in progress, that our 'real country' is still to come and that, until it arrives, constant change and renewal are here to stay.

A new home

'Now the dwelling of God is with human beings, and he will live with them. They will be his people, and God himself will be with them and be their God. He will wipe every tear from their eyes. There will be no more death or mourning or crying or pain, for the old order of things has passed away' (Revelation 21:3–4).

Here we have a far more intimate picture of heaven, reminding us that, however transformative and earth-shattering the actions of God may be, we will not be afraid anymore because we will be in his presence and at home in him. However threatening the concept of change in the Church may feel to us, if the changes are genuinely of God and we are genuinely seeking his presence, we will soon feel at home with the changes themselves. I remember, as a pastor, feeling for those who dreaded seeing their beloved church reordered. For those who had worshipped there for years, there was a genuine bereavement in losing all their familiar furniture and surroundings.

I remember more, however, how quickly and excitedly they embraced the new building as home. Of course, if we hadn't trodden on holy ground and gone about the project carefully, the whole thing could have been a disaster. But when the path of change is planned and processed prayerfully, the outcome can feel more like coming home, and the challenge turns to contentment.

A new city

It shone with the glory of God, and its brilliance was like that of a very precious jewel, like a jasper, clear as crystal. It had a great, high wall with twelve gates, and with twelve angels at the gates. On the gates were written the names of the twelve tribes of Israel. There were three gates on the east, three on the north, three on the south and three on the west. The wall of the city had twelve foundations, and on them were the names of the twelve apostles of the Lamb. (Revelation 21:11–14)

The city, first of all, speaks of safety, security and strength, and reminds us that, however we shape and change the Church, it must always be built on solid foundations and be mindful of its history, theology and doctrines. Sadly, however, the Church has often used this as an excuse to build its doctrinal and cultural walls in unhelpful ways that shut people out and make it almost impossible to enter. The images here speak of easy access and welcome, with several gates on each side of the city. Gates in the scriptures always symbolize opportunities to enter, and here they remind us that there are many opportunities to enter the kingdom of God, and that people can come in from different directions and in many ways into the one city. Although there is only one gospel and only one authentic response, we should never try to stereotype the ways and means by which God works, with whom he works and when.

Shaping the Church for a new generation is a complex and challenging task, but it is a task that we must take up, building many gates for the many cultures we need to reach. Without wanting to push the analogy too far, just as the twelve gates of the city are made out of twelve pearls (v. 21), so we should remember that wherever a person chooses to enter the kingdom of God, that gate, for them, is a pearl that has drawn them to the pearl of great price, the treasure of being a son or daughter of God. Fresh expressions and ancient expressions of church are equally precious in the eyes of God, and both have their place in his purposes. We need many gates with different names, all built with the help and imagination of the same Spirit.

A new garden

On each side of the river stood the tree of life, bearing twelve crops of fruit, yielding its fruit every month. And the leaves of the tree are for the healing of the nations (Revelation 22:2).

This final image reminds us of the remarkable journey that God's people will have taken through human history, beginning and ending with a garden. Driven out of Eden, the human race travels on through many strange new places and experiences, while God's covenant people pass in and out of slavery, in and out of the desert, pioneering, possessing, building and expanding, struggling and conquering, and all the while being redeemed from their own shortcomings and shortsightedness. Eventually, the paths of history lead back to a garden, but this garden is in the heavenly city of God, transformed and reshaped along with its inhabitants.

Following a path of change in the Church should be seen not as straying from our roots, but as travelling ever deeper into the heart of God. The journey itself is bound to take us through some unfamiliar places and may at times feel disorientating, but the promised garden at the end is the embodiment of wholeness and fruitfulness. In fact, for those of us who shape change and change the shape of Church, the ultimate test of success is whether or not we're being fruitful and seeing the fruits of change. At the same time, a lack of fruit in any part of the Church's life will always be an indicator that further change is needed, that the work on the garden is not yet finished.

PAINTING THE PICTURE

It's fascinating and humbling to see how impossible it is to paint a true picture of heaven, but the same applies if we try to paint a definitive picture of a changing Church. Joseph Myers makes the point that so many of our programmed attempts at defining Church are as contrived as using a paint-by-numbers kit.[3] The Church is not a cheap copy of someone else's design. It is a work of art in the making, with many different shades, shapes and colours, and as it moves and inspires us it invites our further participation. In writing this book, I have wanted to reflect that. Instead of prescribing a single 'church by numbers' programme, I have set out a range of principles, so that you can choose what you need for your own design.

As you do this, I hope you'll become like the painter L.S. Lowry. Initially working in obscurity, he painted Salford landscapes with the eye of a local and the heart of a northerner. The extent of his passion and skill were long hidden and sometimes ridiculed, but in time his paintings came to be classified as masterpieces. The shaping of Church has a similar story—happening in secret, often unrecognized, painted by locals but celebrated over time. In all this, my prayer is that change will become a choice to enjoy instead of a challenge to endure, and that we will learn to see it as the finest of art, still in the making and thoroughly down to earth but ultimately speaking of heaven.

———— ✦ ————

MEETING THE CHALLENGE

Looking for heaven

- After reflecting on what the scriptures tell us about heaven, think about how and where God might want you to readjust your investments—of time, energy, money, gifts and so on.

A new universe

- Creativity and change are part of God's character. Would you like to receive more of him in this area? Why?

A new home

- How can we help people to feel more at home with the changes that the Church needs to make?

A new city

- How well built, secure and open is your church in spiritual terms? How many 'gates' does it have?

A new garden

- How much fruitfulness do you see in the garden of your church?
- As you have read this book, what has God been saying to you about your own life and church, and the challenge of change?

✤

CORE VALUES OF ST MARK'S, HAYDOCK

ALL INVOLVED

- from the youngest to the oldest
- in discovering and developing our gifts
- in giving as much as we receive
- in developing a servant culture
- in particular through cells and celebrations

We value

- variety in everything
- boldness in risk-taking
- grace in failing
- strength in weakness
- growth in developing
- training in excellence

We also value

- a willing and generous spirit
- a grateful and encouraging heart

——— ✤ ———

BECOMING DISCIPLES

- from the cradle to the grave
- focused on Jesus
- centred on biblical revelation
- applied practically and personally
- bearing more and more fruit

We value

- learning for the whole of life
- teaching that is systematic and inspirational
- application that enables response
- mentoring that is focused and full of encouragement
- training that is relevant, practical and varied

We also value

- the enquiring mind
- the open heart
- the passionate spirit
- seeking God in all things

——— ✤ ———

CREATING COMMUNITY THAT IS...

- all ages and all types
- welcoming and inclusive
- relaxed and informal

- affirming and empowering
- creative and charismatic
- supportive and safe
- united yet diverse

We value relationships that are

- unconditionally loving
- open and real
- honest and vulnerable

We also value

- mutual acceptance
- submission
- forgiveness
- accountability

———— ✛ ————

DOING EVANGELISM THAT IS...

- true to God's word
- true to the Spirit's leading
- true to our culture (i.e. being relevant)
- true to ourselves (i.e. being natural)
- true to our calling (i.e. being obedient)

We value

- the importance of every Christian taking every opportunity—being intentional, courageous, sensitive and wise

———— ✤ ————

ENCOUNTERING GOD THROUGH THE COMBINED POWER OF...

- word and spirit
- worship and community
- prophecy and prayer
- faith and feeling
- mind and heart
- receiving and sacrifice
- hunger and expectancy
- praise and confession
- waiting and watching
- openness and desire

We value

- variety and flexibility
- contemporary and traditional
- spontaneity and structure

✣

NOTES

Chapter One: Shaping up

1 George Carey, *The Church in the Market Place* (Kingsway, 1995), p. 65.
2 Adrian Plass, *Bacon Sandwiches and Salvation* (Authentic Media, 2007), p. 26.
3 Gordon Bailey, *Moth-balled Religion* (STL, 1972), p. 12.
4 David Watson, *I Believe in Evangelism* (Hodder & Stoughton, 1976), p. 57.
5 Michel Quoist, *Prayers of Life* (Logos Books, 1963), p. 94.
6 Phil Potter, *The Challenge of Cell Church* (BRF, 2001), p. 127.

Chapter Two: Shaping priorities

1 Geoffrey Hanks, *70 Great Christians: The Story of the Christian Church* (Christian Focus Publications, 1992), p. 188.
2 Jim Collins, *Beyond Entrepreneurship* (Prentice Hall, 1992), p. 63.
3 Don Everts, *Jesus with Dirty Feet* (IVP, 1999).
4 Collins, *Beyond Entrepreneurship*, p. 63.
5 The Collins-Porras Vision Framework, from the article 'Organizational Vision and Visionary Organizations', *California Management Review* (Fall 1991).
6 Collins, *Beyond Entrepreneurship*, p. 63
7 Potter, *The Challenge of Cell Church*, pp. 39–40 and Chapters 3—7.
8 Collins, *Beyond Entrepreneurship*, p. 70.
9 Collins, *Beyond Entrepreneurship*, p. 73.
10 Collins, *Beyond Entrepreneurship*, p. 74.

Chapter Three: Shaping people

1   Dr Spencer Johnson, *Who moved my cheese? An amazing way to deal with change in your work and your life* (Vermilion, 1998).
2   John Finney, *Understanding Leadership* (Daybreak, 1989).
3   Malcolm Gladwell, *The Tipping Point* (Abacus, 2000).
4   Frances Hodgson Burnett, *The Secret Garden* (Puffin Classics, 1911), first page of chapter 27.

Chapter Four: Shaping perceptions

1   Isaac Asimov, 'My own view', in Holdstock (ed.), *Encyclopedia of Science Fiction* (Octopus, 1978).
2   Walter Truett Anderson, *The Truth about the Truth* (Tarcher/ Putnam, 1995).

Chapter Five: Reshaping mission

1   Michel Quoist, *Prayers of Life* (Logos Books, 1963), p. 94.
2   The Archbishops' Council, *Mission-Shaped Church* (CHP, 2004).
3   www.freshexpressions.org.uk: click on 'home', then 'welcome'.

Chapter Six: Redesigning church

1   Gerald Coates, *Gerald Quotes* (Kingsway, 1984), p. 65.
2   Neil Cole, *Organic Church* (Jossey-Bass, 2005), p. 100.
3   Christian A. Schwarz, *Natural Church Development Implementation Manual* (British Church Growth Association, 1995).
4   William A. Beckham, *The Second Reformation: Reshaping the Church for the 21st Century* (Touch Publications, 1995), p. 25.
5   Mike Breen and Walt Kallestad, *The Passionate Church: The Art of Life-Changing Discipleship* (Kingsway, 2005).
6   George Lings, *Encounters on the Edge* No. 5: 'Joining the club or changing the rules?' (Church Army, 2000), pp. 12–15.

7   C.S. Lewis, *Mere Christianity* (Fount, 1952), chapter 9, p. 172 (1982 edition)
8   Edward T. Hall, *The Hidden Dimension* (Anchor Books/Doubleday, 1966), pp. 117–124.
9   Joseph R. Myers, *The Search to Belong* (Emergent YS Books, 2003), p. 39.

Chapter Seven: Re-imagining leadership

1   Leonard Sweet, *Summoned to Lead* (Zondervan, 2004), p. 12.
2   John Dominic Crossan, *The Dark Interval: Towards a Theology of Story* (Eagle, 1988), p. 28.
3   Ori Brafman and Rod A. Beckestrom, *The Starfish and the Spider: the Unstoppable Power of Leaderless Organizations* (Penguin, 2006).
4   Fred Drummond, *All That Jazz: Learning to Hear the Kingdom Tune in a New Setting* (Authentic, 2007).
5   Tim Elmore, 'A new kind of leader' in Philip Walker (ed.), *Healthy Church Magazine*, Issue 11 (Healthy Church UK, Autumn 2006), pp. 14–16.

Chapter Eight: All things new!

1   C.S. Lewis, *The Last Battle* (Book Club Associates, 1981), p. 172.
2   David C.K. Watson, *God's Freedom Fighters* (Movement Books, 1972), p. 20.
3   Joseph R. Myers, *Organic Community* (Emersion, 2007), pp. 26–27.

cpas

CPAS is an Anglican evangelical mission agency working with churches, mainly in the UK and Republic of Ireland.

CPAS enables churches to help every person hear and discover the good news of Jesus.

CPAS
Athena Drive
Tachbrook Park
WARWICK
CV34 6NG
01926 458458
info@cpas.org.uk
www.cpas.org.uk

LEADERSHIP PROGRAMME

The Arrow Leadership Programme aims to develop Christian leaders for the Church of the 21st century. It is not merely another course or conference—its aim is 'life transformation'. Over 18 months, Arrow helps participants to grow through teaching, reflection, worship, interaction, application, accountability and fun.

For further information visit www.cpas.org.uk/arrow or call CPAS.